Contents

1 My Interests

 1 Listen and write the number.

a

b

c

d

e

f

___ **a**   reading

___ **b**   painting

___ **c**   acting

___ **d**   playing the guitar

___ **e**   doing martial arts

___ **f**   playing baseball

2   Look at the pictures in 1. Which of the activities do people usually do alone (A)? Which do they usually do with others (O)? Which do they sometimes do both alone and with others (AO)? Write A, O, or AO.

1 _____   2 _____   3 _____

4 _____   5 _____   6 _____

3   Which of the activities in 1 do you do in your free time? Write the numbers.

_____

4   **Match the interests with the school groups. Write the letter.**

Interests

___ **1**   martial arts

___ **2**   acting

___ **3**   writing articles

___ **4**   playing music

___ **5**   building things

School Groups

a   drama club

b   science club

c   school orchestra

d   school newspaper

e   tae kwon do club

5   **What are you good at? What school group do you want to join? Complete the sentences.**

I'm good at _____.

I want to join _____.

What school group could they join?

1   Susan can move really fast.   _____

2   James is good at taking pictures.   _____

3   Elizabeth won a prize for a play she wrote.   _____

4   David's really interested in technology.   _____

5   Anna plays the violin really well.   _____

6   Richard's the best singer in our class.   _____

How did I do?   ☆ ☆ ☆ ☆ ☆

6 Listen and read. Then answer the questions.

Manbury School News Opinion Page

Home | For Teachers | For Students | School Directory | Clubs

DO WHAT'S RIGHT FOR YOU

bbrown

It's a new school year. Everyone is talking about the new after-school clubs because they're fun. You can learn new things and make new friends. But some students aren't interested in joining clubs. They may be shy or scared of groups. These students might be good at singing or playing an instrument, but they like doing these activities alone. They don't want to join clubs, and that's fine.

I'm a shy girl. I enjoy watching sports on TV, painting, and playing my guitar. I'm not interested in joining a sports team, art club, or the school orchestra. My friends were upset with me because I didn't want to join their clubs, so I talked to my mom about it. She said, "It's OK. Be yourself. Do the things you like to do." I want to say to shy children like me, "Do what's right for you. Find friends who are like you. You don't always have to do what everyone else does."

Comments

Silver

I'm shy, too. I always feel bad when my classmates talk about signing up for after-school clubs. I'm glad to know that I'm not the only one.

suki.park

Wow! I love clubs, and I never thought some children might not want to join them. Thanks for writing this. Personally, I don't like doing things alone, so clubs are good for me.

1 What's this newsletter about?

_____

2 Is the newsletter writer interested in joining clubs? Why/Why not?

_____

3 What does she enjoy doing?

_____

7 **What do you think about the newsletter? Write your own comment.**

_____

How did I do? ☆☆☆☆☆

Language in Action

12
8 Listen. Then read and circle **T** for true or **F** for false.

Cathy: Are you interested in joining a club this year, Ben?

Ben: <u>I don't know</u>… I don't have much time. I usually have homework. And when I have free time, I read my manga comics.

Cathy: Manga? Those Japanese comic books? Cool! Hey, did you hear that there's a manga club at school this year?

Ben: <u>No way!</u>

Cathy: Yeah, <u>seriously</u>. You can sign up in Mr. Wang's room.

Ben: Where did you hear about it? When does it meet?

Cathy: Kenna told me about it. I joined yesterday! It meets on Wednesdays and Fridays.

Ben: Oh, good. I can do that.

Cathy: <u>Great!</u> See you there tomorrow.

1 Ben has a lot of free time.   T   F

2 The manga club meets twice a week.   T   F

3 Ben is going to join the manga club.   T   F

4 Cathy hasn't joined the manga club.   T   F

9 Look at **8**. Read the underlined expressions. Match the expressions with their meanings. Write the letters.

___ **1** I don't know.   **a** This is good news.

___ **2** No way!   **b** It's true. It's not a joke!

___ **3** Seriously.   **c** I'm *really* surprised. I can't believe it.

___ **4** Great!   **d** I'm not sure what I want to do.

13
10 Complete with three of the expressions in **9**. Listen and check your answers.

A: Our class is going to Disneyland for our class trip.

B: ¹_____ ! How exciting! When do you leave?

A: Tomorrow morning at 4 a.m.

B: ²_____ ! That's crazy! It's so early!

A: Yeah, ³_____. Four in the morning.

How did I do? ☆ ☆ ☆ ☆ ☆

Grammar

How about <u>joining</u> the baseball team?   OK. I <u>love</u> **playing** baseball.
How about **trying out** for the school play?   Cool. <u>I'm good at</u> **acting**.
How about **playing** a musical instrument?   Good idea. <u>I'm interested in</u> **playing** the trumpet.

11   **Look at the pictures and complete the sentences. Use the correct form of the verbs in the box.**

do tae kwon do   play chess   play soccer   take photos

1   Sue and Keenan both enjoy _____.

2   Sue enjoys _____. Keenan isn't interested in it.

3   Sue has a good camera. She likes _____.

4   Keenan enjoys martial arts. He loves _____.

12   **Complete the dialogs. Circle the correct form of the verbs.**

1   **A:** How about **joins** / **joining** the basketball team?

    B: I'm not sure. I'm not very good at **playing** / **play** basketball.

2   **A:** How about **joining** / **you join** the tae kwon do club?

    B: Great! I love **do** / **doing** martial arts.

3   **A:** How about **tries** / **trying** out for the school play?

    B: I don't know. I'm not very interested in **acts** / **acting**.

4   **A:** How about **goes** / **going** to the new action movie with me on Saturday?

    B: Well, maybe. But I don't really like **watching** / **watches** action movies.

    How did I do? ☆☆☆☆☆

13 Write the questions. Use **How about** and the words in the box.

Do you like playing sports? Yes No
Are you interested in acting? Yes No
Do you like doing math problems? Yes No
Do you enjoy writing stories? Yes No

Nora

| audition for / school play | join / school newspaper team |
| join / science club | try out for / track team |

1 **Paula:** _____
Nora: Good idea! I really enjoy playing sports.

2 **Paula:** _____
Nora: I don't know. I'm not good at acting.

3 **Paula:** _____
Nora: That's a good idea. I'm great at math, and I love doing projects.

4 **Paula:** _____
Nora: Sounds great! I enjoy writing!

14 Complete the sentences about a friend. Use **he** or **she**.

My friend's name is _____. _____ likes _____, and
_____ is good at _____. _____ isn't interested in
_____, but _____ and I enjoy _____.

15 Write answers that are true for you.

1 How about trying out for the soccer team?

_____

2 How about joining the book club?

_____

3 How about auditioning for the school band?

_____

How did I do? ☆☆☆☆☆

16 **Match the words with the definitions. Write the letters.**

___ **1** logical
___ **2** brain
___ **3** imaginative
___ **4** analyze
___ **5** solve
___ **6** creative
___ **7** personality

a good at thinking of new ideas

b the unique combination of traits that characterize a person

c the part of your body that controls how you think, feel, and move

d find the answer to a problem

e examine the details in order to understand something

f good at making new things

g reasonable and sensible

17 **Listen and read. Then circle the correct name.**

Left Brained or Right Brained?

Tom

"I have a left-brained personality. I'm really good at solving math problems. I like to analyze things and to think logically. I like working alone, too. I enjoy writing, but I'm not good at being creative. I'm very organized, so I like listening and taking notes in class. I usually remember the details when I read. As I study, I write things down and make lists. It helps me remember."

Sara

"Honestly, I'm the opposite of Tom. I'm definitely more right-brained than left-brained! So, for example, I'm imaginative and creative. I like making up and telling stories. I love drawing, dancing, and playing music. I enjoy working in groups and solving problems together. Sometimes I talk when I shouldn't in class, and I get distracted when I should be listening. When I study, I draw pictures because it helps me remember.

1 Who likes doing projects in groups?   Tom   Sara

2 Who should try out for the school musical?   Tom   Sara

3 Who should be a school news blogger?   Tom   Sara

4 Who's probably quieter in class?   Tom   Sara

    How did I do? ☆ ☆ ☆ ☆ ☆

18 **Complete the sentences with the words from the box.**

> competition   Olympic   motor vehicle
> variations   event   race course   sport

1   Swimming is a popular _____ at the Olympics.

2   The tug-of-war _____ had a team at each end of a long rope.

3   Hot air ballooning was an _____ sport in 1900.

4   In skijoring a _____ pulls a skier over a race course.

5   My favorite Olympic _____ is sailing.

19 *17* **Listen and read. Then rewrite the sentences so that they are true.**

New Olympic Sport

Did you know that extra fast bike riding is a sport in the Olympics? Bike racing started as an Olympic sport in Athens in 1896. Over the years, there were road races and track races and mountain-bike racing in the Olympic Games. Then, in the 2008 Beijing Games, a bike sport called BMX became a new Olympic sport. It's a very fast and dangerous sport, so competitors have to be fearless to take part!

Both men and women compete in BMX. The bikes they use are light and very strong. They need to be strong enough for all the jumps and ramps, and yet remain light, so the riders can travel as fast as possible. All the races last only forty seconds! If you blink, you'll miss them!

Like any sport, BMX racing has its own special words. The riders have created new words to talk about their sport, such as *bunny hop*. A bunny hop is when a rider's bike goes up in the air. The rider in the picture is bunny hopping. Another special word is *whoop*. A whoop is a small bump in the road. So, the next time you ride your bike, watch out for whoops and don't bunny hop. Stay safe!

1   Only men compete in BMX. _____

2   The bikes are heavy. _____

3   Each race lasts sixty seconds. _____

4   A bunny hop is a small bump in the road. _____

How did I do? ☆☆☆☆☆

Writing | News article

A good news article includes important information about an event. It includes the answers to these questions: *Who* is the article about? *What* is the article about? *When did* the event happen? *Where* did the event happen? *What happened*?

A good news article also gives other information to make the story interesting, but don't forget to answer the questions!

KEY QUESTIONS:
Who?
What?
When?
Where?
What happened?

20 **Read the answers (A). Complete the questions (Q) with Who, What, When, Where, or What happened.**

1 Q: _____? You're all dirty!

A: I slipped and fell in the mud!

2 Q: _____ does the club meet?

A: It meets in the science lab.

3 Q: _____ 's that over there?

A: That's my science club leader.

4 Q: _____ does the science club meet?

A: It meets on Mondays after school.

5 Q: _____ do you do in science club?

A: We build things and play fun games.

21 **Write a news article. Use the information in the chart. Add interesting information.**

Who?	What ?	When?	Where?	What happened?
people who enjoy acting	audition for the musical *Peter Pan*	last Monday after school	in the auditorium	more than 20 students auditioned

Interesting information:
Everyone was nervous. Mr. Bannister's going to post the results on the school website.

_____

_____

_____

_____

How did I do? ☆☆☆☆☆

Review

22 Where do these activities usually take place? Write them in the correct column.

> act on stage   join the track team   play baseball
> play the guitar   play soccer   write articles

Inside	Outside
_____	_____
_____	_____
_____	_____
_____	_____

23 Write questions with **how about** and the words in parentheses. Then look at the pictures and complete the answers.

1 Peggy: Carla, _____

_____?

(try out for / soccer team)

Carla: No way! You know I only play

_____.

2 James: Olivia, _____

_____?

(sign up for / school newspaper)

Olivia: Great idea! I really enjoy

_____.

3 Marco: _____

_____?

(join / the school band)

Daniel: No, I can't play an instrument, but

I'm interested in _____.

Maybe I'll join the drama club.

How did I do? ☆ ☆ ☆ ☆ ☆

2 Family Ties

Language in Context

1 Match the pictures with the sentences. Write the number.

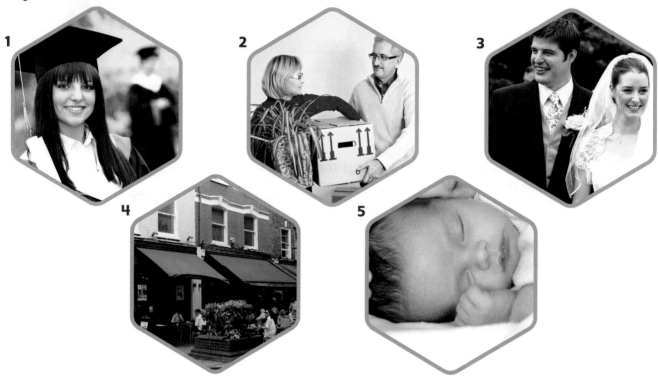

____ **a**   The couple got married.

____ **b**   The student graduated from college.

____ **c**   The family moved to a new house.

____ **d**   The family opened a restaurant.

____ **e**   The baby was born at 5 a.m.

2   Answer the questions about your family. Circle Yes or No.

Last year:

1	Did your family open a store?	Yes	No
2	Did you move to a new home?	Yes	No
3	Did a family member graduate from college?	Yes	No
4	Was a new family member born?	Yes	No
5	Did a family member get married?	Yes	No

3 Match and complete the phrases. Write the words.

1 graduated

2 moved

3 got

4 opened

5 was

a _____ to a new place

b _____ from business school

c _____ born

d _____ a store

e _____ married

 4 Listen to the events in Ken's life. Then number the timeline in order and write the events.

25

Timeline of Ken's Life

Age 25 _____

Age 44 _____

Age 21 _____

Age 0 _____

Age 28 _____

THINK BIG

Complete the sentences with *aunt, brother, sister,* or *uncle.*

1 My mom's sister is my _____.

2 My dad's brother is my _____.

3 My aunt is my dad's _____.

4 My uncle is my mom's _____.

How did I do? ☆ ☆ ☆ ☆ ☆

5 Listen and read. Then answer the questions.

My Amazing Family

My name is Theresa, and I have an unusual and amazing family. We're superheroes! We can do amazing things, and we like to help people.

My mom was born in Venice, and she moved to Barcelona in 1996. My dad was born in Barcelona. He met my mom there when they both helped save people in a house fire. They got married in 2000 and had three children soon after that. I'm the oldest child, and I have a younger brother, Tomas, and a baby sister, Tara. Tomas is eight. I'm stronger than him. I can pick up a car! But Tomas is faster than me. He can run a kilometer in less than 15 seconds! That's really fast! Tara is incredible! She can make herself very, very small – sometimes smaller than a peanut. That's why we call her "Peanut". I love my family because we're always doing exciting things.

1 Why is this family amazing?

_____

2 Where was Theresa's mom born?

_____

3 Where did Theresa's parents meet?

_____

4 Who's the oldest child in the family?

_____

5 Why does the family call Tara "Peanut"?

_____

6 Answer the questions.

1 What special power would you like to have? Why?

_____

2 What are you going to do with your special power?

_____

How did I do? ☆ ☆ ☆ ☆ ☆

Language in Action

7 **Listen. Then circle the correct answers.**

Will: Oh... this is a great picture! What a cute baby!

Deb: Guess who... ?

Will: No! That's not you! Is it?

Deb: Yes... that's me. That's the day I was born.

Will: <u>That's nice.</u> But... what happened?

Deb: <u>What do you mean?</u>

Will: You were so much cuter then!

Deb: <u>Ha! Ha! Very funny.</u> My mother says I was the cutest baby in the world.

Will: <u>Well, I don't know...</u> but you were pretty cute.

Deb: Thanks.

1 Who is the baby in the picture?

  a someone in Will's family   **b** Deb

2 Will ___ when he says that Deb was cuter when she was a baby.

  a is serious   **b** is joking

3 Deb's mom said that she was the cutest baby in the world. Will ___.

  a agrees   **b** doesn't really agree

8 **Look at 7. Read the underlined expressions. Match the expressions with their meanings. Write the letters.**

___ **1** That's nice.   **a** I don't understand what you're talking about.

___ **2** What do you mean?   **b** That's not funny.

___ **3** Ha! Ha! Very funny.   **c** I don't think that's exactly true.

___ **4** Well, I don't know...   **d** I like it.

9 **Circle the correct expression.**

1 **A:** That's a picture of my brother.

  B: **That's nice. / Well, I don't know.** You look just like him.

  A: Yes, I do because we're twins!

2 **A:** That's the day we moved.

  B: **What do you mean? / Ha! Ha! Very funny.**

  A: We moved from New York to Ohio.

  B: I didn't know that!

How did I do?

Grammar

We **went** to Los Angeles <u>when</u> I **was** eight.
<u>When</u> they **were** kids, they **lived** in Mexico City.

She **moved** to Florida three years <u>ago</u>.
A few months <u>later</u>, she **got** a new job.

10 **Find and circle eleven past tense verbs.**

was f h a d g w got n were u y t went m l i v e d o p moved t found k j f bought w started q c worked m

11 **Look at 10. Write the past tense form of the verbs.**

be	was / were	**have**	
buy		**live**	
find		**move**	
get		**start**	
go		**work**	

12 **Complete the paragraph. Use the correct form of the verbs in 11.**

My mom and dad ¹_____got_____ married when they ²_____ 24.
They ³_____ with my dad's parents because they ⁴_____
to save money to buy their own house. They both ⁵_____ long
hours at their jobs. A few years later, they ⁶_____ a house. That
⁷_____ 15 years ago. They ⁸_____ into the house on my
mother's birthday. I ⁹_____ born a year later!

How did I do? ☆ ☆ ☆ ☆ ☆

Sue's **taller than** Yoko and Mark.
Sue's **the tallest** person in our class.

31
13 Listen and number the family members.

14 Look at the picture. Complete the sentences. Use the correct form of the words in parentheses.

1 (tall) Joan is _____tall_____.
Ben is _____ Joan.
Ben is _____ child.

2 (young) Maria is _____.
Maria is _____ Joan and Ben.
Maria is _____ child.

3 (long) Maria's hair is _____
Ben's hair. Joan's hair is _____
hair of all.

Maria   Joan   Ben

15 Think of a good friend. How are you different? Write sentences. Use the words in the box.

| big   new   old   strong   tall |

1 _____

2 _____

3 _____

16 **Read the family descriptions. Circle the correct animal.**

1 These animals live in packs.	**wolves**	**elephants**
2 The females eat first.	**elephants**	**lions**
3 These animals live in troops.	**chimpanzees**	**wolves**
4 The males live on their own.	**elephants**	**lions**
5 The leaders are called alphas.	**wolves**	**chimpanzees**
6 These animals can cry.	**lions**	**elephants**

 17 **Complete the text with the words in the box. Then listen and check.**

> dad   male   Female   prides   families   children

Good and Bad Dads in the Animal Kingdom

Just like your mom, your dad is a special and important person in your family. Think of all the things that your dad does for you. Many dads work hard to pay for the things that their families need. They also do many things at home to help take care of their children.

Fathers are important in the animal kingdom, too. They take care of their families and some even take care of other families. But some fathers are better than others.

1 Lions live in social groups called _____. _____ lions find food and take care of the children. Male lions aren't great dads. They like to sleep a lot.

2 Seahorses have big _____. Seahorses can have 1,000 babies at a time. The male seahorse is a good _____. He carries the eggs in his tail for three weeks until the baby seahorses are born.

3 Emus don't usually live in families, but _____ emus are great dads. The male emu builds a nest for his _____ all by himself. He sits on the eggs until the baby emus are born. During this time, he doesn't eat or drink!

How did I do? ☆ ☆ ☆ ☆ ☆

35

18 Listen and read. Match paragraphs 1–4 with pictures a–d. Who eats Fairy Bread on their birthday?

Special Birthdays

Do you celebrate your birthday? Is there a special tradition in your family or in your culture for birthdays? Many cultures around the world celebrate birthdays – in many different ways. Some cultures celebrate by giving treats to the birthday boy or girl. Other cultures celebrate by doing something special that symbolizes the child's special day. Read on to find out more about how some children around the world celebrate their birthday.

1 In Nigeria, first, fifth, tenth, and fifteenth birthdays are very important. Many parents have big parties for their children and more than 1,000 people come. They eat a lot – sometimes a whole roasted cow!

2 A lot of Brazilian children have fun birthdays. Some parents decorate the house with brightly-colored banners and flowers. Brazilians also pull on the ear of the birthday boy or girl. They pull once for each year.

3 On the first birthday of all Hindu children in India, the parents shave the top of their child's head. When they are older, they have birthday parties. They wear new clothes and give thanks to their parents by touching their parents' feet. At school, the birthday child gives chocolate to classmates.

4 Australian children have very sweet birthdays! They eat Fairy Bread. This is a slice of bread and butter covered with small sugary sprinkles called *hundreds and thousands*.

19 Read 18 again and circle **T** for true or **F** for false.

1	Fifth, tenth, fifteenth, and twentieth birthdays are important in Nigeria.	T	F
2	Sometimes people in Nigeria roast a cow for a special birthday.	T	F
3	Brazilian parents sometimes decorate the house on their child's birthday.	T	F
4	Brazilians pull twice on a child's ear for each year of his or her birthday.	T	F
5	When Hindu children in India turn one, their parents shave the top of their heads.	T	F
6	Australian children have fairy cakes on their birthdays.	T	F

How did I do? ☆ ☆ ☆ ☆ ☆

Writing | Autobiography

An autobiography describes the important events in your life and when they happened. The events are in the order they happened. The information often includes:

- when and where you were born
- places you lived
- things you did
- your family and friends
- special memories
- your interests.

 20 **Read Adele's autobiography. Add events from the chart. Use the correct form of the verbs.**

Dates	Events
1988	be born in London, England
1991	start singing
2006	write my first successful songs
2009	win a Grammy Award
2011	have throat surgery
2009 to the present	start donating to charities

My Life

My name is Adele. My full name is Adele Laurie Blue Adkins. ¹_____ in 1988. I'm an only child. I don't have any brothers or sisters, so my mom and I are very close. I ²_____ in front of my mom's friends when I was only three. I loved music and ³_____ when I was at the BRIT School for Performing Arts and Technology. I was about 18 years old. Three years later, ⁴_____ . That was in 2009. I ⁵_____, but I'm fine now and continue to sing and receive awards for my work. In 2009, I ⁶_____ that help sick children and families of sick children and to charities that help musicians in need.

 21 **In the Student's Book, you were asked to write a story about your life. Now write a different, imaginary story about your life. Complete the chart below and use it to help you write.**

Date	Event
_____	_____
_____	_____
_____	_____

How did I do? ☆ ☆ ☆ ☆ ☆

22 **Complete the sentences. Use the correct form of the verbs in the box.**

| be born | buy | get married | move | start |

Notes about my family

1   My brother _____ a new car last month. He is so happy.

2   I miss my grandma and grandpa. A year ago, they _____ away, and now they live in Monterey.

3   My cousin _____ art school last year. He is a really good artist.

4   I have a new baby brother. He _____ a few weeks ago. He looks like me!

5   When my parents _____, they were very young. They made a beautiful couple.

23 **Complete the sentences. Use when, ago, or later and the correct form of the verbs.**

When?	Age 16	Age 17	Age 18	Age 19	Age 21
What happened?	learn to drive	get a part-time job	start college	buy first car	graduate

1   Jack ___learned___ to drive ___when___ he ___was___ 16.

2   He _____ a part-time job _____ he _____ 17.

3   _____ he _____ 18, he _____ college.

4   One year _____, he _____ his first car. He _____ 19.

5   He _____ from college two years _____ and now he works at a bank.

24 **Complete the dialog. Use the correct form of the words in parentheses.**

A: Tell me about your family, David.

B: Well, I have three sisters, Jen, Beth, and Kim. Jen is _____ (old) of the three. Beth is _____ (young). And Kim is in the middle.

A: Really?

B: Yeah. And guess what. Beth is _____ (tall) in my family!

How did I do? ☆☆☆☆☆

3 Helping Others

1 **Which activities do you see in the pictures? Write the numbers.**

1 2 3

4 5 6

___ **a** have a cake sale   ___ **b** tutor or teach someone   ___ **c** make posters

___ **d** clean up a place   ___ **e** walk to raise money   ___ **f** wash cars

2 **Look at 1. Which fundraising activity would these people be best at doing? Write the numbers.**

1 Maria likes cleaning up. She's good at organizing things.

2 Carlos loves math. He's really good at explaining math problems.

3 Jason likes being outdoors. He loves running, swimming, and bike riding.

4 Emma loves baking cookies and cupcakes. She enjoys baking for other people.

3 **Unscramble and write the words.**

1

rta ifar

_____

2

ekca lesa

_____

3

ehva a tccnoer

_____

4

eakm a diove

_____

5

Walk-a-thon on Monday

Walk to Raise Money

meak soteprs

_____

6

Bank School helps others by

erwti na riatlce

_____

41
4 **Complete the sentences with the words in 3. Then listen and check.**

1 Why don't we have a _____ next week at school? I can make cookies, and you could make a cake.

2 Sara knows how to use the video camera. She can _____ to tell people about our event.

3 We could _____ to make money. A lot of us love to play music.

4 We could _____ and hang them up around school.

5 Let's draw and paint some things and sell them at an _____.

6 Someone could _____ for the school website.

THINK BIG

Grade 6 at your school wants to raise money for a local children's hospital. What could they do? How could they tell people about it?

_____

_____

How did I do? ☆☆☆☆☆

5 **Listen and read. Then answer the questions.**

On Monday, September 25th at 2:30 p.m., Alex in Grade 6 wrote:

WE NEED MONEY!

Listen, everyone. As you know, our school needs a lot of things. We need new computers for the computer lab, a new freezer for the kitchen, and new chess sets for the chess club. There will soon be some fundraising activities. Fundraising events are often boring, I know. But I think we could be more creative and do some fun things. I talked to some students, and here are some of the best ideas:

- **Karaoke competition with children and parents:** We can sell tickets to each contestant, and parents and children can compete against each other.

- **Temporary tattoos:** We could sell tattoos of cartoon characters and other fun things.

- **Students vs. teachers sports events:** I'd love to see this! We could play basketball or ping-pong. Any other suggestions for sports?

- **Parents' spelling quiz:** Let's have our parents spell words! Could your parent win?

What do you think? Let me know. We can talk to our teachers and see if they like the ideas. Maybe we could come up with a fundraising plan for this year that's really fun! ☺

COMMENTS

arichards
Great ideas! I'll help you! Talk to you later.

carrie_thomas
The karaoke night is a fantastic idea! I know my parents would be interested.

1 What's the blog about?

_____

2 What does the writer think about past fundraising activities?

_____

3 What does the writer think about the fundraising plan for this year?

_____

6 **What new fundraising ideas do you have? Add a comment.**

_____

How did I do? ☆ ☆ ☆ ☆ ☆

Language in Action

7 Listen. Then circle the correct answers.

Pete: That car looks great! <u>What's up?</u>

Mary: Oh, thanks. We're having this car wash to raise money for our science club. We're going to buy materials for our science projects.

Pete: <u>It's too bad</u> you don't have many people or cars.

Mary: Yes. I guess a lot of people don't realize we're doing this here.

Pete: I have an idea. Taylor and I could make signs and hold them up over there so more people will stop.

Mary: <u>What a great idea!</u> We didn't think about that!

1 What is the science club going to do with the fundraiser money?

a buy materials for science projects   **b** give the money to charity

2 How many people and cars are there?

a a lot   **b** not a lot

3 What are Taylor and Pete going to do?

a help wash cars   **b** make signs and hold them up

8 Look at **7**. Then circle the best meaning for each expression.

1 What's up?

a How are you?   **b** What are you doing?

2 It's too bad.

a It's great.   **b** It's not good.

3 What a great idea!

a I like your idea a lot.   **b** I'm not sure what your idea is.

9 Complete with two of the expressions in **8**.

1 A: Hey, Leslie. _____?

    B: I'm studying. What are you doing?

2 A: I know what we could do to make money. We could sell raffle tickets.

    B: _____. I like it a lot!

How did I do? ☆☆☆☆☆

Grammar

How **could** we raise money for our club?	We **could** have a car wash.
How much **could** they charge to wash one car?	They **could** charge $10 for a small car. For a bigger car, they **could** charge $15.

10 **Complete the questions. Use How could or How much could. Then match the questions with the suggestions. Write the numbers.**

1 Let's have a class trip fundraiser.
_____ we raise with a fundraiser?

___ **a** We could write articles about it in the school newspaper.

2 _____ we charge for our winter concert tickets?

___ **b** I think we could raise a lot of money.

3 _____ we tell people about the fundraiser?

___ **c** We could probably ask for $5.00 a ticket.

11 **Read the sentences. Complete the sign-up sheet with the correct names. Then complete the sentences. Use could.**

The Art Club Book Sale Sign-Up Sheet

Team 1: Collect books Monday after school	Team 2: Make posters on Tuesday after school	Team 3: Sell books on Saturday	Team 4: Clean up on Saturday at 4:00
1 Jil	1 Gina	9:00–11:00: Tanya	1 Brendan
2 Samantha	2 Ben	11:00–1:00: _Tina_	2 Jeff
3 _____	3 _____	1:00–3:00: Candy	3 _____

1 Tina is free on Saturday at 11:00. She _could sell books_____.

2 Paul is free after school on Monday. He _____.

3 Sally is free on Tuesday after school. She _____.

4 Mario is free on Saturday at 4:00. He _____.

12 **Look at 11. How and when could you help?**

_____

How did I do? ☆☆☆☆☆

| Are you **going to have** a concert? | Yes, we **are**. |
| How **is she going to** tell people about it? | She**'s going to** make posters. |

13 **Complete the sentences. Use am/is/are going to.**

Fifth Grade News

Hi everyone!

This is a busy week! Don't forget! Our class car wash is this Saturday! We
¹_____ meet in front of the school at 7:30 in the morning. Please be on
time. Bring a towel and an extra set of clothes – you ²_____ get very wet.
I ³_____ bring snacks. Please bring something to drink.

Also, Carol ⁴_____ make posters this Thursday. I hope you can join her
and help out. And Jeremy ⁵_____ hand out flyers to parents.

Now we need YOU. Join us! How ⁶_____ we _____ make
this a success without you? Can you help? Let me know. And remember to tell your parents and
family. I know we ⁷_____ have a great time and make lots of money!

See you there!

Mrs. Hendricks

14 **Look at the students' schedule for next week. Complete the questions and answers. Use am/is/are going to and the activities in the chart.**

KIDS HELPING – WEEKLY CALENDAR		
	Me	**Peter and Hugo**
make a video of the glee club	✓	
do a long walk for charity		✓

1 A: How _____ you _____ get kids interested in joining the glee club?

B: I _____.

2 A: How _____ Peter and Hugo _____ raise money for charity?

B: They _____.

How did I do? ☆ ☆ ☆ ☆ ☆

15 **Match the words with the definitions. Write the letters.**

___ **1** font

a pictures

___ **2** images

b the style of the letters

___ **3** design

c how the information is organized

___ **4** layout

d the way the font and images look

___ **5** effective

e successful

48
16 **Listen and read. What does a successful ad need to have?**

Effective Advertisements

Advertisements tell people about a product and make people want to buy it. Think of an ad that you think is effective. What makes it good? Is it the picture or is it the text? Maybe you like the way the images and font look or how the information is organized? A successful ad has an interesting design, images, and fonts. These things add to the impact of the ad. If the layout is good, the message is more effective. And if the message is very effective, then it's a great ad!

A

Come to the Grade 6 talent show!
The music club is going to have a talent show next Saturday to raise money for new instruments.
Please come. It's going to be lots of fun!
The talent show starts at 5:30. Tickets are only $5.00.

B **Come to the Grade 6 talent show**

We're raising money for new instruments.
Saturday evening.
Show starts at 5:30.

It's going to be lots of fun!

Tickets are only $5.00.

17 **Look at the ads in 16. Which one is more effective? Read and check A or B.**

	A	B
1 The font is clear and easy to read.	☐	☐
2 The images tell me a lot about the talent show.	☐	☐
3 The layout is attractive.	☐	☐
4 The poster has an interesting design.	☐	☐
5 This poster makes me want to buy a ticket.	☐	☐
6 The information is clear and well organized.	☐	☐

How did I do? ☆☆☆☆☆

18 Complete the sentences with the words in the box.

> depressed   residents   population   retirement

1 The _____ in many countries is getting older.

2 Older people can become _____ if they spend too much time on their own.

3 Older people live in _____ homes when they become too old to look after themselves.

4 We call the people who live in a home _____.

19 Look at page 35 of the Student's Book. Circle **Yes** or **No**.

1 There are around 7 billion people over the age of 65 in the world.   **Yes / No**

2 People will live twice as long by 2050.   **Yes / No**

3 Volunteers visit people over the age of 70 in Tokyo.   **Yes / No**

4 Volunteers encourage older people in Tokyo to meet people outside their homes.   **Yes / No**

5 Older people in the Intergenerational Learning Center in Seattle often spend time with children.   **Yes / No**

6 Students in the Netherlands can live in a retirement home for a small amount of rent.   **Yes / No**

20 How could young people help older people in your country?

We could _____

_____

_____

_____

_____.

How did I do? ☆☆☆☆☆

A well-written letter is well organized and contains clear ideas. It usually includes:

- the **date**
- a **greeting**, such as *Dear Mr. Smith*,
- the **body** of the letter
- a **closing**, such as *Sincerely*, or *Best wishes*,
- your **signature** (your name).

The letter in this unit offers suggestions. When you write a letter that gives a suggestion, the body of the letter talks about:

- your idea or suggestion
- how people can carry out the idea
- why the idea is important.

21 **Write the parts of the letter.**

> body   closing   date   greeting   signature

1 _____ May 10, 2017

2 _____ Dear Mr. Green,

3 _____ I think that the school should raise money to help the Houses for All charity. This charity builds homes for homeless families. We could raise money for this charity. We could collect coins and raise money that way or we could organize cake sales to raise money.
This project is a good one because all children deserve a good home. We can help. Please think about this idea.

4 _____ Sincerely,

5 _____ Teresa Lee

22 **Look at 21. Circle the answers in the letter.**

1 What's the suggestion?

2 How can people carry out the idea?

3 Why is the idea important?

23 **Write a letter to your teacher. Suggest a plan to raise money for a charity.**

How did I do? ☆☆☆☆☆

Review

24 How can these students raise money for their school fair? Write suggestions with could.

1 I'm Maria. I have a lot of books, but I don't need them.

2 I'm Fred. I'm really good at painting T-shirts.

3 I'm Eric. I have a video camera, and I enjoy making videos.

4 I'm Gaby. I really enjoy writing.

1 Maria _____.

2 Fred _____.

3 Eric _____.

4 Gaby _____.

25 Complete the dialog. Use am/is/are going to.

A: How ¹_____ we ²_____ raise money for computers at school?

B: I have a plan. We ³_____ organize a contest.

A: And how ⁴_____ you ⁵_____ tell people about the contest?

B: I ⁶_____ make big posters and put them up all over school.

A: How ⁷_____ the contest ⁸_____ help raise money?

B: Maybe we could ask students to buy a ticket to be in the contest.

A: Well, I don't know… What kind of contest ⁹_____ you ¹⁰_____ have?

B: We ¹¹_____ have an online writing contest. Children can write a paragraph titled: *Why we need computers at school.* That's a great idea, isn't it?

A: That's silly! The school doesn't have computers! Children can't write online.

B: Oh. OK.

How did I do? ☆☆☆☆☆

1 Look at the pictures. Write the words. Add your own words on the extra line.

My Interests

1 _____
2 _____
3 _____
4 _____
5 _____

Family Ties

1 _____
2 _____
3 _____
4 _____
5 _____

Helping Others

1 _____
2 _____
3 _____
4 _____
5 _____

2 **Think of a famous person or a cartoon character. Complete the information about him or her.**

Name _____	
Interests	He or she is interested in: _____ He or she is good at: _____ He or she likes: _____
Family Ties	Here are some family events in his or her life: _____ _____ _____
Helping Others	Here's a way he or she could help: _____ _____ Here's what he or she is going to do: _____ _____

3 **Think about a song your person could like. Use 1 and 2 to help you. Write a letter to your person about it. Explain why you chose this song.**

_____
_____
_____
_____
_____
_____
_____
_____
_____
_____

4 Shopping Around

Language in Context

1 Match the pictures with the places. Write the numbers.

1

2

3

4

5

6

___ **a** mall

___ **c** craft fair

___ **e** electronics store

___ **b** department store

___ **d** shoe store

___ **f** flower shop

2 Where do you like to shop? ✓ your answers.

☐ clothing store

☐ bookstore

☐ flower shop

☐ video game store

☐ music store

☐ jewelry store

3 Look at 1 and 2. Which of these places are there in your neighborhood? Circle them.

57

4 Listen and number the presents.

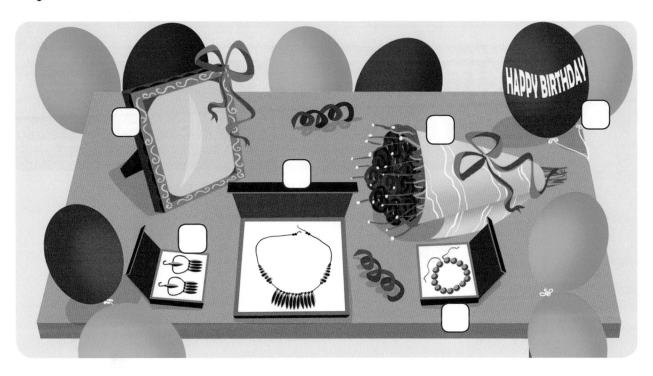

5 Where could you buy these presents? Circle the correct answers.

1 a turquoise necklace   **a** a craft fair   **b** an electronics store

2 silver earrings   **a** a flower shop   **b** a department store

3 a beaded bracelet   **a** a mall   **b** a music store

4 balloons   **a** a mall   **b** a craft fair

5 a bouquet of roses   **a** a bookstore   **b** a flower shop

6 a handmade picture frame   **a** a craft fair   **b** a sports store

Think about some presents for your family.

1 Your sister loves jewelry. What kind of jewelry could you buy her for her birthday? _____

2 Your mom loves flowers. What kind of flowers could you buy her for Mother's Day? _____

How did I do? ☆☆☆☆☆

6 **Listen and read. Then ✓ the correct person.**

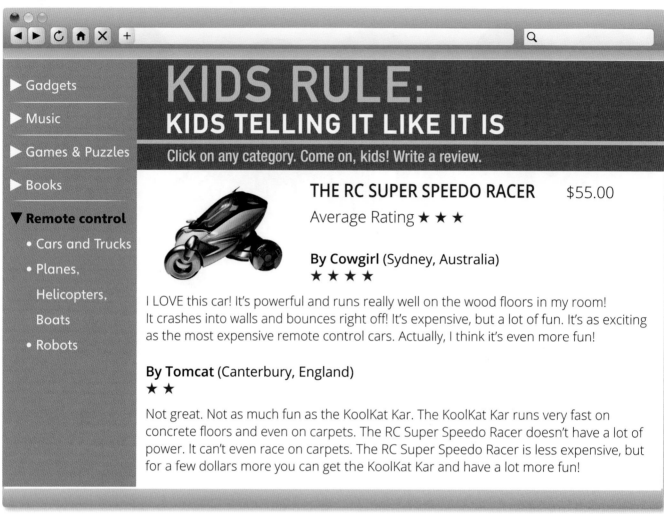

▶ Gadgets

▶ Music

▶ Games & Puzzles

▶ Books

▼ Remote control

• Cars and Trucks

• Planes, Helicopters, Boats

• Robots

KIDS RULE:
KIDS TELLING IT LIKE IT IS

Click on any category. Come on, kids! Write a review.

THE RC SUPER SPEEDO RACER $55.00

Average Rating ★ ★ ★

By Cowgirl (Sydney, Australia)
★ ★ ★ ★

I LOVE this car! It's powerful and runs really well on the wood floors in my room! It crashes into walls and bounces right off! It's expensive, but a lot of fun. It's as exciting as the most expensive remote control cars. Actually, I think it's even more fun!

By Tomcat (Canterbury, England)
★ ★

Not great. Not as much fun as the KoolKat Kar. The KoolKat Kar runs very fast on concrete floors and even on carpets. The RC Super Speedo Racer doesn't have a lot of power. It can't even race on carpets. The RC Super Speedo Racer is less expensive, but for a few dollars more you can get the KoolKat Kar and have a lot more fun!

	Cowgirl	Tomcat
1 Who likes the RC Super Speedo Racer?	☐	☐
2 Who thinks the RC Super Speedo Racer isn't powerful?	☐	☐
3 Who thinks the RC Super Speedo Racer is less exciting than the more expensive remote cars?	☐	☐
4 Who thinks the RC Super Speedo Racer is expensive?	☐	☐
5 Who likes racing powerful cars that can race on carpets?	☐	☐

7 **Answer the question.**

Which car would you like to buy: the RC Super Speedo Racer or the KoolKat Kar? Why?

_____

How did I do? ☆ ☆ ☆ ☆ ☆

Language in Action

62

8 Listen. Then answer the questions.

Jen: <u>How about</u> this one? It got some really great reviews. Look.

Eddie: <u>Oh yeah</u>? Is it as nice as yours?

Jen: <u>Yeah</u>... It's a really good MP3 player, and it's the least expensive one at this store.

Eddie: <u>Yeah, but</u> it's $85! I don't have that much money.

Jen: Yes, but look. It's on sale! Let's see, it's only $60. It has four gigabytes of memory. And it comes with a free case.

Eddie: Wow! The design is really cool, too. It's perfect!

Jen: Oh, no! There's only one problem.

Eddie: What?

Jen: It's already sold out.

Eddie: <u>Oh, man!</u>

1 Who knows more about MP3 players, Jen or Eddie? _____

2 Does Eddie need to buy a case for the MP3 player? _____

3 Why doesn't Eddie buy the MP3 player? _____

9 Look at 8. Read the underlined expressions. Match the expressions with their meanings. Write the letters.

___**1** How about... ?   **a** I'm really disappointed!

___**2** Oh, yeah?   **b** I know, but...

___**3** Yeah.   **c** What do you think of... ?

___**4** Yeah, but...   **d** Really?

___**5** Oh, man!   **e** Yes.

10 Complete with three of the expressions in 9.

A: ¹_____ going to the craft fair now? There's a big one today.

B: ²_____ Where is it?

A: It's in the park, near school.

B: Great. Maybe I can find a birthday present for my brother.

A: ³_____.

How did I do? ☆☆☆☆☆

Grammar

The blue shoes are expensive.

The red shoes are **more** expensive **than** the blue shoes.
The black shoes are **the most** expensive of all.

The red shoes are not **as** expensive **as** the black shoes.
The blue shoes are **less** expensive **than** the red shoes.
The blue shoes are **the least** expensive of all.

11 Look at the ratings. Circle the correct answers.

Movie Reviews Category: Sci Fi

The Story	Horrible ★	Boring ★ ★	OK ★ ★ ★	Interesting ★ ★ ★ ★	Amazing ★ ★ ★ ★ ★
The Acting	Terrible ★	Disappointing ★ ★	OK ★ ★ ★	Great ★ ★ ★ ★	Extraordinary ★ ★ ★ ★ ★
Popularity	Bomb ★	Not Popular ★ ★	OK ★ ★ ★	Very Popular ★ ★ ★ ★	Extremely Popular ★ ★ ★ ★ ★

	Story	Acting	Popularity
Robots of the Universe	★ ★ ★ ★ ★	★ ★	★ ★ ★ ★
Princess of Evil	★ ★ ★ ★	★ ★ ★	★ ★ ★ ★ ★
The Pirates	★	★ ★ ★ ★ ★	★ ★ ★

1 *The Pirates* is **less** / **more** popular than *Princess of Evil*.

2 The story of *Princess of Evil* is **less** / **more** interesting than the story of *The Pirates*.

3 The acting in *Princess of Evil* is **less** / **more** extraordinary than the acting in *Robots of the Universe*.

4 *The Pirates* is **the most** / **the least** popular movie.

5 The story of *Robots of the Universe* is **the least** / **the most** amazing.

12 Look at the ratings in 11. Then complete the sentences with more/less... than or the most/the least.

1 The story of *Robots of the Universe* is _____ amazing _____ the story of the *Princess of Evil*.

2 The acting in *Robots of the Universe* is _____ extraordinary of all the movies.

3 The story in *The Pirates* is _____ boring of all.

How did I do? ☆ ☆ ☆ ☆ ☆

13 **Complete the sentences. Use as... as or not as... as and the words in parentheses.**

1 The black jeans are _____ (fashionable) the blue jeans.

2 The black jeans are _____ (cheap) the blue jeans.

3 The blue jeans are _____ (baggy) the black jeans.

4 The black jeans are _____ (popular) the blue jeans.

5 The blue jeans are _____ (comfortable) the black jeans.

> The price of those sneakers is **too** high.   The price isn't low **enough**.
> The jeans are **too** small.   The jeans aren't big **enough**.

14 **Look at the picture. Circle the correct answer.**

1 My brother wears really baggy jeans. The blue jeans ___ for him.

   a aren't baggy enough   **b** are too baggy

2 I like colorful pants. Those black jeans ___ for me.

   a aren't colorful enough   **b** are too colorful

3 I usually wear white shirts with my jeans. That shirt ___ for me.

   a isn't bright enough   **b** is too bright

How did I do? ☆☆☆☆☆

15 **Read and complete the puzzle with the words in the box.**

coins
livestock
metal
paper
shells
trade

ACROSS

3 Exchange one thing for another

5 Cows and goats

6 Round metal money

DOWN

1 Bank notes are made of this.

2 This is very shiny – silver is one type of this.

4 Some animals live in these.

 16 **Complete the text with some of the words from 15. Then listen and check.**

The Idea for Paper Money

Long ago, people didn't use bank cards, paper money, or coins to buy things. They bartered with ¹_____ and grain, exchanging them for the things they needed. Over time, people started using other things as money, such as cowrie ²_____. They exchanged the shells for food, animals, and other goods. Then ³_____ coins were made and, finally, paper money. The story of paper money is a fascinating one. The use of bank notes started in the Tang Dynasty. The Tang Dynasty existed in China from AD 618–907.

Before Chinese people used paper money, they used coins. The coins were round and had a square hole in the middle. They kept their ⁴_____ on a rope, so the more coins they had on the rope, the heavier the rope would be. Rich people found that their ropes of coins were too heavy to carry around easily. So what did they do? They left their strings of coins with someone they trusted, and that person wrote down the amount of money he was keeping for them on a piece of paper and gave it to them. When the rich man wanted his money, he took the piece of paper to that trusted person, and he got his coins back. This was a good idea, don't you think? Eventually, ⁵_____ bank notes were created, and people began to use them instead of ropes of coins.

How did I do? ☆☆☆☆☆

66

17 Read and complete. Then listen and check.

| haggle | browse | price | experiences | vendor | expensive |

Shopping Is Fun!

Not everyone enjoys shopping. But, for those that do enjoy it, there are different shopping
¹_____ around the world. Some people like to ²_____ and buy things for the cheapest price. Others just like to ³_____ and not buy anything. For some, shopping is the chance to dress up as a character when they visit their favorite store.

How to shop in Chatuchak Market, Bangkok

Chatuchak Market is a great place to bargain. Everyone bargains here. When you bargain, you try to pay a lower
⁴_____ for something. Here's an example. You want to buy a hat. The hat costs $20. You say to the vendor, the person who sells the hat, "I want to pay $10." The ⁵_____ says, "That's too cheap. How about $15?" You say, "Definitely not! That's still too
⁶_____. How about $12?" The vendor says, "OK, $12." Because you bargained, you just paid $8 less for the hat!

Bargaining is a good skill to have when you shop in some places. You can buy things for less money, and this means you can buy more things.

18 Read 17 again and circle T for true or F for false.

1 Everyone loves to shop.   T   F

2 There are lots of different shopping experiences.   T   F

3 When you browse, you don't buy anything.   T   F

4 You can't bargain at Chatuchak Market.   T   F

5 When you bargain, you want to pay less for something.   T   F

6 Bargaining isn't a useful skill.   T   F

How did I do?

Writing | Product review

A good product review describes what is good and bad about a product and gives a recommendation. A recommendation tells the readers if they should buy the product.

Here are ways to say if a product is good or bad:

Good

It's the best.
They're worth the money.
It's great.

Bad

It's terrible.
They're not worth the money.
It isn't great.

Here are ways to give a recommendation:

I definitely recommend this product.
This product isn't great but [say why some people might like it].
I don't recommend this product because...

Remember to explain your ideas.

19 **Read the product review. Answer the questions. Write the sentence numbers.**

[1]I bought my Wrap-Arounds at Cheap Charlie. [2]They aren't great headphones, but they're good for people who don't have a lot of money. [3]You can buy more expensive headphones and get more amazing sound, but why? [4]I think they're worth the money, especially if you don't need to hear extraordinary sound. [5]I recommend Wrap-Arounds because they offer good sound for little money.

Which sentence explains...

1 who would like the headphones?   ⬜

2 that the headphones are worth the money?   ⬜

3 if you should buy the headphones?   ⬜

20 **Choose a gadget you have or want. Write a review.**

_____

_____

_____

_____

_____

TIPS

To write a good review, you need to decide these things:

1 Do you like the product or no[t]? Why/Why not?

2 What's good or bad about it?

3 Is it worth the money?

4 Will you recommend it or no[t]?

How did I do? ☆ ☆ ☆ ☆ ☆

Review

21 **Write the words in the correct column.**

bracelet   clothing store   craft fair   digital camera   earrings
flower shop   headphones   MP3 player   necklace

Jewelry	Gadgets	Places
_____	_____	_____
_____	_____	_____
_____	_____	_____

22 **Look at the ratings. Complete the sentences. Write more/less popular than and the most/the least popular.**

★★★★★   ★★★   ★★★★

1   The turquoise necklace is _____ the beaded bracelet.

2   The beaded bracelet is _____ the silver earrings.

3   The turquoise necklace is _____ of them all.

4   The beaded bracelet is _____ of them all.

23 **Write the sentences. Use too or not... enough and the words in parentheses.**

1   These shoes look like boats on my feet. They're _____ (big).

2   This digital camera costs a lot of money. It's _____ (expensive).

3   I can't hear the video. It's _____ (loud).

4   These headphones always break. They're _____ (strong).

How did I do? ☆☆☆☆☆

5 Vacation Time

Language in Context

1 Which vacations do you see in the pictures? Write the numbers.

1
2
3
4
5
6

___ biking in the forest

___ lying on the beach

___ hiking in the mountains

___ kayaking down a river

___ skiing in the snow

___ rafting on a lake

2 Look at 1. Which vacation would you like the best? Which vacation would you like the least? Rank the vacations and write their numbers in the chart.

The least	👍👍	👍👍👍	👍👍👍👍	👍👍👍👍👍	The most

3 Write the words in the correct rows.

> a helmet   a life jacket   a map   a warm jacket   a water bottle
> a windbreaker   insect repellent   sunglasses   sunscreen

useful clothing	
useful for eyes	
useful for skin	
useful for safety/health	

4 Look at 3. Complete the sentences.

1 I'm wearing _____ because there are a lot of insects in the woods.

2 Take _____. You'll get thirsty on the hike.

3 When you go horseback riding, wear _____. You could fall.

4 I'm glad we took _____ on our bike trip. We almost got lost.

5 It was very cold in the mountains, so I wore _____.

6 The captain of the boat gave me _____ because the water was rough and dangerous.

7 I didn't put on enough _____ at the beach, and now I have a sunburn.

8 When you walk on the beach in the winter, it can be windy and wet. Be sure to wear _____.

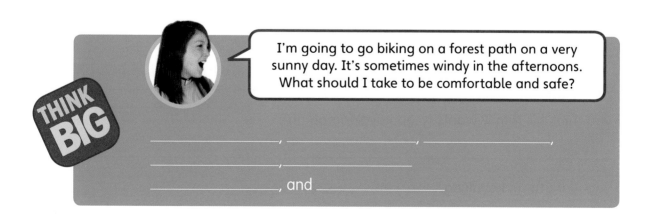

THINK BIG

I'm going to go biking on a forest path on a very sunny day. It's sometimes windy in the afternoons. What should I take to be comfortable and safe?

_____ , _____ , _____ ,

_____ ,

_____ , and _____

How did I do? ☆☆☆☆☆

5 **Listen and read. Then answer the questions.**

A Family's Kayaking Trip

Joe felt awful when he woke up. His head hurt. His stomach hurt. His ears hurt. He was sad because his family was going kayaking soon. His mom looked at him and said, "Sorry, Joe, you're too sick to go with us. You're going to stay at home with Grandma." Joe was angry! It wasn't fair!

His family said goodbye and left. Joe was staring at the TV when his grandma came in. She said, "Don't worry, Joe. You'll go kayaking another day."

Joe stared at the ceiling. He was thinking about his family. They were probably having a wonderful time. He closed his eyes and pictured them. They were in their kayaks on the river, laughing and having fun. There were deer and rabbits on the river banks and birds everywhere.

He was sleeping when his family returned. He woke up as they came into his room. They looked miserable. His mom said, "We had a terrible time. We all got mosquito bites. I fell and hurt my arm on the way to the river. Your sister fell into the river when she got out of her kayak. Your dad hit his head on a tree branch hanging over the river. You're very lucky that you stayed at home."

1 What did Joe's family do?

_____

2 Why didn't Joe go with his family?

_____

3 How did Joe imagine his family's day?

_____

4 Why was Joe surprised when he saw his family?

_____

6 **Answer the questions. Explain your answers.**

1 Do you think Joe still wants to go kayaking?

_____

2 Do you think his family wants to go kayaking again?

_____

3 Do you want to go kayaking?

_____

How did I do? ☆☆☆☆☆

Language in Action

7 Listen. Then circle the correct answers.

Eve: So how did your vacation go?

Gina: It was terrible. On the second day, we went shopping in a small town. I was pretty excited at first. One shop had great souvenirs. You know, T-shirts and magnets, stuff like that.

Eve: I bet you got something wonderful.

Gina: Well, I had my eye on a really cute pair of earrings. But while I was shopping, I lost my wallet. By the time I found it, all the shops were closed!

Eve: Aw, that's too bad. But I guess you saved a lot of money that way!

Gina: Ha! Ha! Very funny!

1 Did Gina have a good time?

    a Yes, she did.

    b No, she didn't.

2 Did Gina really think Eve was funny?

    a Yes, she did.

    b No, she didn't.

8 Look at 7. Circle the correct answers.

1 Eve asks, "How did your vacation go?" What does she want to know?

    a How did Gina go on vacation?   **b** What happened on Gina's vacation?

2 What other "stuff like that" can you buy at a souvenir store?

    a postcards, tourist books, and maps   **b** stoves, refrigerators, and desks

3 What does Eve mean when she says, "I bet"?

    a I guess.   **b** I know.

4 Gina "had her eye on" earrings. What did she want to do?

    a She wanted to buy them.   **b** She looked at them closely.

5 When Eve says, "too bad," what does she mean?

    a I'm sorry you didn't feel well.   **b** I'm sorry the stores were closed.

9 Complete with three of the expressions in 7.

A: Last week I went to a great Mexican market. I ¹_____ some cool scarves there. ²_____ you'd like them. They were in your favorite colors.

B: What else did they have there?

A: Local food and traditional pottery... ³_____. It was all amazing!

How did I do? ☆☆☆☆☆

Grammar

What **was** he **doing** when he got hurt?	He **was** horseback **riding** when he got hurt.
What happened while they **were hiking**?	They got lost while they **were hiking**.

10 Find and circle the 8 verbs in the iguana's tail. Use the verbs to answer the question.

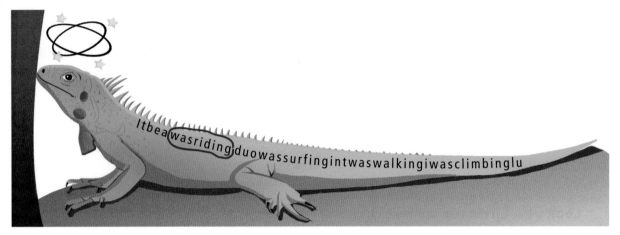

What was the iguana doing when it got hurt?

1 It ____was riding____.

2 _____.

3 _____.

4 _____.

11 Match the two parts of the sentences. Write the letters.

___ **1** While Jack was hiking in the snowy mountains

___ **2** Sue and Ben sang songs

___ **3** Steve was riding his bicycle

a he got lost and very cold.

b when he rode into a tree.

c while they were kayaking down the river.

12 Look at 11. Answer the questions.

1 What was Jack doing when he got lost in the mountains? _____

_____

2 What happened while Sue and Ben were kayaking? _____

_____

How did I do? ☆ ☆ ☆ ☆ ☆

Was he biking when it started to rain?	Yes, he was./No, he wasn't.
Were you swimming when you got sunburned?	Yes, I was./No, I wasn't.

13 **Complete the questions with the correct form of wear. Then write the answers.**

1 Was he wearing
sunglasses when you saw him on
the beach?

Yes, he was.

2 _____
life jackets when they got wet?

_____.

3 _____ a jacket
when she climbed up Big Mountain?

_____

4 _____
a hat when you saw her?

_____

5 _____ a helmet
when he fell off his bike?

_____

6 _____
sunscreen when you saw her at
the beach?

_____

How did I do? ☆☆☆☆☆

Content Connection | Math

14 **Read and ✓.**

1 when you add numbers together

a multiplication ☐   **b** addition ☐

2 someone who buys things

a customer ☐   **b** receipt ☐

3 something you buy

a item ☐   **b** price ☐

4 when you add the same number several times

a addition ☐   **b** multiplication ☐

5 a list of what things cost

a souvenir ☐   **b** price list ☐

6 when you find the answer using math

a calculation ☐   **b** sell ☐

15 **Read and complete. Then listen and check.** 78

| chips | customers | items | multiplication |
| price list | sunburned | sunscreen | water |

Jim's Problem

Oh, no! I on
have $9.33!

BEACH SHACK

CHIPS	$1.09
WATER	$1.25
SUNSCREEN	$6.99

One day, Jim was lying on the beach when he realized he was
[1]_____. He was also hungry and thirsty. So he went to Beach
Shack. He looked at the [2]_____ to see what to buy. He picked
up five [3]_____: three bags of [4]_____, a bottle of
[5]_____, and some [6]_____. But when Jim went to
pay, the girl who was serving the [7]_____ said, "That's $11.51,
please." Oh, no! Jim didn't have enough money! He wasn't very good
at addition and [8]_____. He solved his problem by putting
back two bags of chips.
How about you? How would you solve the problem?

How did I do? ☆ ☆ ☆ ☆ ☆

16 **Match the words with the definitions. Write the letters.**

___**1** expedition

a very interesting

___**2** guide

b the area around the North Pole

___**3** arctic

c especially

___**4** fascinating

d a trip around a place with a guide

___**5** particularly

e someone whose job is to show a place to tourists

___**6** guided tour

f a long trip that is carefully planned

80
17 **Listen and read. Match headings A–E with paragraphs 1–5. Write the numbers.**

A Different Types of Family Vacations ___

B Cultural Activities on a Staycation ___

C Going on a Staycation ___

D Advantages of a Staycation ___

E Example of a Staycation ___

A Staycation in Italy

1 Every year, families all over the world go on vacation. Vacations are wonderful times to be with family and explore new places and cultures. Many families like visiting other countries while on vacation and learning about the history of a particular country from guides. Other families enjoy discovering parts of their own country and learning more about their own history and culture. Sometimes families like to stay at home. They don't like to travel, but they do like to explore new places and cultures. How can they do both? These families can go on a "staycation."

2 Here is how a staycation works. Your family decides on a culture and a country that they want to know more about. They do research and find out about that country's music, crafts, food, art, and other things. Then they try to create the culture in their home during the vacation.

3 For example, say that your family wants to learn more about Italian culture. Your family would do research and find out about the following things:

- popular Italian food
- popular Italian music
- popular Italian stories
- Italian art
- Italian vacations and other events
- the Italian language

4 During the staycation, your family would plan activities to do together, to learn about Italian culture. You might eat at Italian restaurants, go on a guided tour at a museum to study Italian artists, and see Italian movies.

5 Staycations are a great way to enjoy your family, stay at home, and learn fascinating things, too!

How did I do? ☆☆☆☆☆

Writing postcards is a great way to share your vacation with friends and family. Choose a postcard with a picture of a place you visited or plan on visiting. On the other side, there is space for the address of the person you are writing to and space for a short note about the picture or your trip. A postcard includes (in this order):

- the **date** (*July 5th*)
- a **greeting** (*Hi* or *Dear...*)
- a **body** with information about the place or your plans (*I'm having a great time! We went to the beach yesterday.*)
- a **closing** (*See you soon!* or *I miss you!*)

Don't forget to sign your name. You want your friends and family to know the postcard comes from you! And on the right side of the card, don't forget to put the full address of the person you are writing to (name, street address, town/city, postcode, country).

18 **Write the parts of the postcard.**

1 _____ August 22nd

2 _____ Dear Aunt Edna,

3 _____ I'm so happy. I'm having a wonderful time with my family in South Africa. The weather's warm. The animals in the safari park were amazing. Tomorrow we're going to Cape Town.

4 _____ See you soon!

19 **Imagine you are visiting a place you know well. Answer these questions.**

What's the name of the place? _____

What are you doing there? _____

What exciting things have you seen? _____

Are you enjoying yourself? Why/Why not? _____

20 **Use your answers in 19. Write a postcard to your teacher about that place.**

_____
_____
_____
_____

How did I do? ☆☆☆☆☆

Review

21 **Find and circle the words. Then write the words in the correct group.**

| biking | campsite | helmet | rafting | skiing | tent |

```
c  s  d  x  d  g  d  v  m  c
r  a  f  t  i  n  g  r  e  k
n  g  m  t  f  a  s  g  k  u
g  o  t  p  l  k  i  n  g  n
e  b  l  o  s  k  i  i  n  g
u  i  g  t  u  i  g  l  d  i
l  k  o  i  f  g  t  e  n  t
t  i  i  h  e  l  m  e  t  g
o  n  w  r  i  t  i  n  g  a
n  g  a  e  n  t  t  g  i  t
r  c  f  o  i  a  s  f  n  o
```

Vacation activities

_____

_____

_____

Vacation things

campsite _____

_____

_____

22 **Complete the sentences. Use the correct form of the words in the box.**

| driving | looking | putting on | reading |

1 We _____ to the amusement park when it started to rain.

2 My dad _____ at a map when he saw the bear right in front of him!

3 My mom got sunburned while she _____ her book on the beach.

4 I _____ sunscreen when I got stung by a bee.

23 **Read. Then answer the questions.**

Yesterday morning, Tim and Jill were swimming in the lake.
Yesterday afternoon, Jill went hiking while Tim was at a picnic.

1 Was Tim hiking yesterday morning?

_____

2 Were Tim and Jill swimming in the lake yesterday?

_____

How did I do? ☆☆☆☆☆

Unit 5 **53**

6 The Future

Language in Context

1 Which of these inventions do you think will be common in stores by 2020?
✓ your answers.

1 **3D video games on sale!** Be in the game!

2 Spend your next family vacation **on the moon!** Book your next trip on the Moon Cruiser.

3 **Buzz Around on Super Highways!** Buy the new Fly Car.

4 **Chameleon Clothes!** Clothes that Change Color! Buy now and save!

5 Live in a Smartie House with Robot Help! Never clean up again!

⬭ 3D video games   ⬭ Fly Car   ⬭ Robot Help

⬭ Moon Cruiser   ⬭ Chameleon Clothes

2 Look at 1. Which inventions would you like to buy? Circle the numbers.

1   2   3   4   5

3 What can you do with these electronic devices? ✓ your answers.

	smartphone	MP3 player	tablet	laptop
You can...				
1 make phone calls				
2 write essays and do homework				
3 listen to music				
4 watch movies and play games				
5 text people				

4 Unscramble the words. Use the words in **3**.

1 She listens to music on her _____. 3PM lpyrae

2 They read stories on their _____. ptmsrahneo

3 He watches movies on his _____. taetbl

4 He does his homework on his _____. ptlopa

Which electronic device is most useful for doing homework? Why?
_____

Which electronic device is best for playing games? Why?
_____

How did I do? ☆ ☆ ☆ ☆ ☆

5 **Listen and read. Then answer the questions.**

Jenny's Bad Morning

Jenny, a Grade 6 student, was sleeping when her bed started shaking. While the bed was shaking, a strange voice said, "Jenny, wake up! Time to go to school!" "You'll wake everybody up! Stop shaking and talking!" Jenny said. "Sorry," said the bed.

"I'm hungry," said Jenny. "Good morning, Jenny," a robot chair said. She sat on the robot and patted it. The robot carried her to the kitchen. "What would you like for breakfast, Jenny?" asked the fridge.

Jenny said, "Crunchy Crisp Cereal and toast, please." Five seconds later, the fridge opened up and put a bowl of cold cereal in front of her, and the toaster added hot toast with butter.

After breakfast, Jenny sat on the robot chair again, and it took her to her room. Jenny got dressed. "These clothes are too tight," said Jenny. The robot said, "Clothes, be bigger." The clothes got a little bigger. "Perfect!" said Jenny.

It was time for school. Jenny's mom said, "Hurry up, Jenny, get in the Fly Car." "Fly Car? No one rides in Fly Cars anymore," thought Jenny. Jenny wanted to use a Flying Suit to fly her to school. Her mom shook her head. "Sorry, you can't use a Flying Suit until you're 12." Jenny got in the Fly Car. She wasr happy. She hated being 11! She thought, "I want to be 12! It'll be so much more fun."

1 How did Jenny wake up?

_____

2 Who made Jenny's breakfast?

_____

3 How did Jenny get to school?

_____

4 Did Jenny like the Fly Car? Why/Why not?

_____

6 **Answer the question.**

Would you like Jenny's life? Why/Why not?

_____

_____

How did I do? ☆ ☆ ☆ ☆ ☆

Language in Action

7 **Listen. Then answer the questions.**

Mom: Jason, <u>come on</u>. It's time to get ready for school.

Jason: Oh, Mom. Do I have to?

Mom: Yes! Get your books ready while I <u>log on</u> to your virtual classroom.

Jason: OK. <u>Whoops!</u> I'm almost late for my English class!

Mom: At least you don't have to take the bus for an hour to school any more. Your teacher's right here for you all the time. You just need to <u>turn</u> your computer <u>on</u>!

Jason: Yes. But this robot teacher is stricter than the human ones were!

Mom: That's good. Maybe you'll learn more!

1 Where does Jason go to school?

_____

2 How does Jason start classes with his teacher?

_____

3 Why does Jason prefer human teachers to robot teachers?

_____

8 **Look at 7. Read the underlined expressions. Match the expressions with their meanings. Write the letters.**

___ **1** come on

___ **2** log on

___ **3** Whoops!

___ **4** turn on

a Oh no!

b Hurry! Let's go.

c start using a computer program

d start using a machine

9 **Complete with the expressions in 8.**

Mom: ¹_____, Emma. It's three o'clock. You'll be late for the soccer game.

Emma: Mom! The game was at two! I've missed it!

Mom : ²_____! Sorry, Emma. Never mind, it's raining anyway.

Emma: That's OK. I'll ³_____ to our soccer website and play online.

Mom: Good idea. I'll ⁴_____ the lights for you. It's getting dark.

How did I do? ☆ ☆ ☆ ☆ ☆

Grammar

| Do you think we**'ll have** cars 100 years from now? | Yes, we **will**. But cars **won't have** drivers! They**'ll use** computers. |
| | No, we **won't**. We**'ll have** spaceships. |

 10 Look at the pictures. Complete the sentences. Use **will** or **won't**. Then listen and check.

1 Next year smartphones _____ look the same as they do today. In the future you _____ wear your phone on your wrist.

2 In the future we _____ carry heavy, square tablets anymore. We _____ have tablets that are light and roll up.

3 People probably _____ listen to music on an MP3 player in the future. With one Patchster patch near each ear, you and your friends _____ be able to listen to the same music at the same time.

11 Complete the questions. Use **will** or **won't**. Then answer the questions.

1 Do you think computers _____ roll up in the future?

_____

2 Do you think smartphones _____ be as smart as you?

_____

3 Do you think robots _____ clean your room for you?

_____

How did I do? ☆ ☆ ☆ ☆ ☆

Who will use video messaging in the future?	**Anyone** with a computer and internet access will use video messaging.
Who will send letters to communicate with friends in the future?	**No one/Nobody** will send letters to communicate with friends. **Everyone/Everybody** will use email. Well, **someone** might write a letter!

12 Read the class survey. Then circle the correct words.

Mrs. Brown's Class Survey – Which activities will we do in 2030?

Will we...	Percentage of people who said "yes"
1. drive solar-powered cars?	100%
2. read paper books?	10%
3. go to Mars on spaceships for a vacation?	0%
4. use non-digital cameras?	0%
5. send paper birthday cards?	20%

1 ___ will drive solar-powered cars.

(a) Everybody   **b** Someone

2 ___ will read paper books.

a No one   **b** Someone

3 ___ will use non-digital cameras. They'll take pictures with digital cameras and smartphones.

a No one   **b** Someone

4 ___ who likes to write will send paper birthday cards. Everyone else will send electronic cards.

a Nobody   **b** Anyone

13 Circle the sentences in 12 that you agree with. Write about one sentence that you don't agree with. Explain why.

I don't think that _____ because _____

_____.

How did I do? ☆☆☆☆☆

14 **Match the words with the definitions. Write the letters.**

___ **1** assistive

___ **2** capabilities

___ **3** surgical

___ **4** procedures

___ **5** socially

___ **6** complicated

a skills

b medical

c processes

d with people

e difficult

f helpful

94

15 **Listen and read. Then complete the chart.**

Tomorrow's Robots

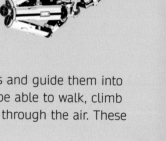

We all know that robots will be part of our future. They will help people do things that they're unable to do. That's good, isn't it?

Firefighter Robots

One day, there will be robots that fight fires. Human firefighters will control the robots and guide them into burning buildings. One type of robot will look like a real firefighter. These robots will be able to walk, climb up ladders, and see through smoke. Another type will look like a snake, able to move through the air. These will help firefighters find people trapped in small places.

Running Robots

There might also be some robots that look like animals. They'll probably have four legs and be able to run very fast. They'll have bigger back legs than front legs so that they can jump, too. These robots will probably help police catch criminals. They'll catch the criminals because they'll be able to run faster than humans.

Jumping Robots

This robot won't look like an animal or person, but it'll do amazing things. It'll have wheels that move it from place to place. What's amazing about this robot is that it'll be able to jump very high. In fact, it might be able to jump over walls or onto rooftops. It'll help police see if there are dangerous things or people there.

	Robot	What will it be able to do?	Who will it help?
1	Firefighter Robot		
2	Running Robot		
3	Jumping Robot		

How did I do? ☆ ☆ ☆ ☆ ☆

96
16 **Read and complete. Then listen and check.**

| generations   extinct   endangered   speakers   language |

Saving Languages: Now and Long Ago

Did you know that at least one language becomes ¹_____ in the world every month? Languages are disappearing fast, and experts believe that in less than 100 years, there will be only half of the languages left in the world that there are today. But there are some attempts to preserve ²_____ languages. For example, the Khang language and culture is one of the most endangered dialects in Vietnam. There are only 4,000 known speakers, and they don't have a written ³_____ . UNESCO (United Nations Educational, Scientific, and Cultural Organization) decided to help keep the Khang language and culture from disappearing. UNESCO workers wrote down Khang traditions, developed an alphabet, prepared materials for teaching the language in classes, and trained local ⁴_____ to teach those classes. Now, Khang speakers will be able to pass on the language to their children for ⁵_____ to come. This seems like an effective way to preserve a language, doesn't it?

17 **Read 16 again and circle T for true or F for false.**

1 In 100 years, there will be twice as many languages as there are today.   T   F

2 The Khang language always had an alphabet.   T   F

3 The Khang people are studying their language in classes today.   T   F

4 Teaching the Khang language to young people will make the language endangered.   T   F

How did I do? ☆☆☆☆☆

A diary is a special notebook. People often write about their day in this notebook. They write about the things that happened, and they often write about their feelings or thoughts during the day. Many people like writing in their diary every day. Some people share their diary entries. Some people write only for themselves. A diary entry is similar to a letter. It includes:

- a **greeting** (*Dear Diary, Hello*)
- an **opening sentence**. It usually describes the topic of your entry. (*I'm very happy today.*)
- the **body**. It includes information about the topic.
- a **closing** (*Goodnight, Love, Bye*)
- your **name**

18 **Label the parts of the diary entry.**

1 _____ Dear Diary,

2 _____ We learned about the future in school today.

3 _____ I started thinking about my life in the future. In five years, everyone in my class will be in high school.

I hope I'll have a boyfriend, and that he'll be nice! I won't be able to drive, but I hope that Mom and Dad will let me stay out late. I'm tired now, so I'll say goodbye.

4 _____ Goodnight,

5 _____ Pat

19 **Look at 18. Circle the correct answers.**

1 What comes after the greeting?   **a** a period (.)   **b** a comma (,)   **c** nothing

2 What comes after the closing?   **a** a period (.)   **b** a comma (,)   **c** nothing

3 What comes after the writer's name?   **a** a period (.)   **b** a comma (,)   **c** nothing

20 **Imagine your life six years from now. Write a diary entry about a day in your life. Use 18 and 19 to help you.**

_____

_____

_____

_____

_____

How did I do? ☆☆☆☆☆

Review

21 **Look at the chart. Then complete the sentences. Use will or won't.**

My predictions about the year 2030	I don't think we will have these things! Bye-bye!	I think these things will definitely be here!
1 **text friends**	with cell phones	with wrist phones
2 **write assignments**	on laptops – parents might use them	on tablets
3 **listen to music**	on MP3 players	on Patchster-like devices
4 **buy items**	mostly online using computers	mostly online using electronic gadgets

1 I think people _____ with cell phones. We _____ with wrist phones.

2 We _____ on tablets in 2030. We _____ on laptops.

3 In the future, we _____ on MP3 players. We _____ on Patchster-like devices.

4 I think we _____ mostly online using our electronic gadgets.

   We _____ online using computers.

22 **Look at 21. Complete the sentences. Use Everybody or Nobody.**

1 _____ will use cell phones.

2 _____ will write assignments on laptops.

3 _____ will listen to music on a Patchster-like device.

4 _____ listen to music on MP3 players.

23 **Answer the questions. Use your own ideas.**

1 Do you think people will carry umbrellas in the future? Why/Why not?

_____

2 Do you think we'll read only electronic books in the year 2025 instead of paper books? Why/Why not?

_____

How did I do? ☆ ☆ ☆ ☆ ☆

1 Look at the pictures. What are they? Write the words.

Shopping Around

1 _____

2 _____

3 _____

4 _____

Vacation Time

1 _____ 2 _____

3 _____ 4 _____

The Future

1 _____

2 _____

3 _____

4 _____

2 Find or think of a song that talks about shopping, a vacation, or the future. Complete the chart.

Song title	
Singer	
Is the song in English? What language is the song in?	
What's it about?	
Why do you like listening to this song?	
Is it the most popular song now?	
What were you doing when you first heard it?	
Do you think it'll be popular next year?	

3 Write a review of the song for your school newspaper. Use the information in 2 to help you.

_____
_____
_____
_____
_____
_____
_____
_____
_____

7 What's That?

Language in Context

1 Look at the pictures. Match the gadgets with their uses. Write the letters.

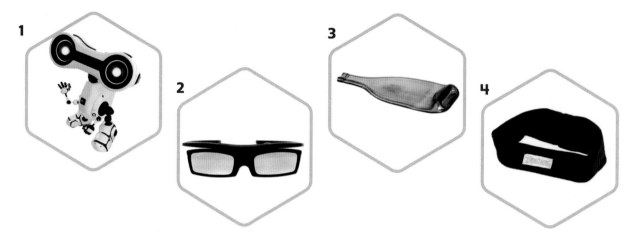

1   2   3   4

___ **Picture 1** This is used for...

a listening to music. You wear this headband to listen to music comfortably, even while you sleep. It's a music headband.

___ **Picture 2** These are used for...

b doing research. You ask it questions and it tells you the answers. It helps you find information. It's Robo-pedia.

___ **Picture 3** This is used for...

c watching movies. You put on these glasses and watch movies that only you can see. They're movie theater glasses.

___ **Picture 4** This is used for...

d drinking. You can fill it up with water and drink it. When you're finished, you can roll it up and put it away. It's a roll-up bottle.

2 Which gadgets in **1** do you like? Rate them. **1 = It's amazing! 2 = It's cool. 3 = It's OK. 4 = It's boring/not interesting.**

a Robo-pedia ___

b roll-up bottle ___

c movie theater glasses ___

d music headband ___

3 Match the old things with the modern things. Write the numbers.

1  2  3  4

a  b c d

___ ___ ___ ___

104
4 Read and complete the sentences. Use the words from the box. Then listen and check.

| cell phone smartphones games console instant camera radio gadgets |

Today ¹_____ are used for talking to people, taking pictures, playing games and listening to music and the news.

Before smartphones people needed different ²_____.

A ³_____ was mostly used for talking to people. An ⁴_____ was used to take pictures. A ⁵_____ was used to play games and a ⁶_____ was used for listening to music and the news.

THINK BIG

What do you think about the future of these items? Will we still use them in the future? Why/Why not?

| maps cars watches |

_____

_____

How did I do? ☆☆☆☆☆

5 Listen and read. Then answer the questions.

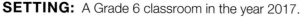

CAST

| Ann, Jim (classmates) | Miss Albany (teacher) |

SETTING: A Grade 6 classroom in the year 2017.
[The class finds a time capsule that the school made in 1990. They open it and are looking at the things inside it.]

Ann: [picking up a thin square object] Look at this. What is it?

Jim: [takes it from her and looks at it carefully] I'm not sure. It's plastic, and it has a metal rectangle on it.

Ann: Hmm… I think it was used for watching movies on a computer.

Jim: I don't think so. I don't think people could watch movies on computers in 1990.

Ann: You're right.

Jim: [picking up a thick rectangular object] And what's this? It's some kind of small machine.

Ann: [presses one of the buttons and it starts working] Hey, it's an old music player. [Ann puts the headphones to her ears]

Jim: [putting his hands over his ears] Oh, no! I don't want to listen to old music!

Ann: [laughing] Someone's going to say the same thing about our music in the future. I kind of like this music. I'm going to take it to my grandpa. He might remember this kind of music.
[A teacher enters]

Jim: [holding up the thin square object] Hello, Miss Albany. What's this?

Miss Albany: Oh, that's a floppy disk. People used them to keep information on from a computer. That way they had the information even if their computer didn't work.

Jim: I see.

Ann: It's fun looking at these old things.

1 What did Ann pick up?

_____

2 What did she think it was used for?

_____

3 Did Jim like the music?

_____

4 What did people use the square object for?

_____

6 Answer the questions.

How old does something have to be for you to think it is "old"? Why?

_____

How did I do? ☆☆☆☆☆

109

7 Listen and read. Circle **T** for true or **F** for false.

Iris: What's in the box?

Laura: It's not a box. See? It doesn't open. My grandpa brought it back from China when he went there many years ago.

Iris: Let's see. It's hard and looks like it would break if you dropped it.

Laura: Well, it would! It's ceramic, like the plates and dishes we use for eating.

Iris: OK. But what is it? What's it used for?

Laura: You won't believe it, but it's a pillow!

Iris: A pillow? But it's so hard!

Laura: A long time ago, women in Asia had very beautiful hairstyles that took a lot of work to create. They didn't want to ruin them by sleeping on a soft pillow. So they just rested their necks on a ceramic pillow like this one. It was used for keeping their hair in place.

Iris: Gosh! That doesn't sound very comfortable.

1 The object is a pillow made of plastic. **T F**

2 It was used when women were sleeping. **T F**

3 Iris thinks it's a good pillow. **T F**

8 Look at 7. Read the underlined expressions. Match the expressions with their meanings. Write the letters.

___**1** See?

___**2** You won't believe it.

___**3** Let's see.

___**4** keep (their hair) in place

a It's surprising.

b Look closely.

c keep (their hair) from getting messy

d Let me think.

9 Complete with the expressions in 8.

A: What were those bones used for?

B: ¹_____. Now I remember. ²_____, but those bones were used for a children's game called Knucklebones!

A: How did women in ancient Greece ³_____ their clothes ⁴_____?

B: Well, look at this picture. ⁵_____? They wrapped a piece of cloth around themselves and used pins or belts.

How did I do? ☆☆☆☆☆

Grammar

What's it **used for**? It's **used for/was used for** listening to music.
What **was** it **used for**? It's **used to/was used to** listen to music.

10 **Match and write the letter.**

___**1** A wireless headset is used for

___**2** A cell phone is used to

___**3** A games console is used to

___**4** A radio is used for

a play video games.

b making phone calls.

c listening to music.

d make phone calls.

11 **Look and read. Answer the questions with** used for **or** used to.

| keeping shoes on | listen to music | playing video games | tell time |

1

A: What are they used for?

B: They're used to listen to music.

2

A: What are they used for?

B: _____

3

A: What's it used for?

B: _____

4

A: What's it used for?

B: _____

How did I do? ☆☆☆☆☆

What is it?	I'm not sure. It **may** be a small plate. It **might** be a candy dish.

12 What do you think these old things are? Use the words from the box and may or might to write sentences.

abacus   egg beater   gramophone   washboard

1

It may be a gramophone.

2

3

4

13 Look at the items in 12. What do you think they were used for? Write sentences with used to.

1 _____

2 _____

3 _____

4 _____

How did I do? ☆ ☆ ☆ ☆ ☆

14 **Complete the chart. Use the words from the box.**

> candle   cash register   combustion engine   plumbing

How do the inventions help people?	Invention
1 We can easily take a shower and wash dishes and clothes.	
2 We can travel by vehicles on land, water, and air.	
3 We can see at night when the lights go out.	
4 Stores can keep their money safe.	

 15 **Read. Then answer the questions.**

Everyday Inventions

Who do you think of when you hear the word *inventor*? Do you think of Thomas Edison, the inventor of the light bulb, or Karl Benz, the inventor of the gas-powered car?

Not all inventors are world-famous. In fact, we don't know the names of a lot of inventors who invented some of the small useful things we use every day. For example, everyone knows about the bendable straw. But does anyone know the name Joseph Friedman? In 1937 he invented the bendable straw. Joseph's brother owned a soda store. One day Joseph was watching his small daughter drink a milkshake from a long straw. The straw was long and she couldn't reach the end of it easily with her mouth. You may not think this is a problem, but Joseph did! He said, "Let's see. I'll put a screw into the straw, and wrap floss around it on the outside of the straw." He tried it and then he took the screw out. The straw could bend, and the bendable straw was born.

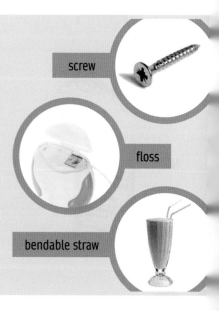

screw

floss

bendable straw

1 Who was with Joseph Friedman at his brother's store? _____

2 What problem was she having? _____

3 What did Joseph Friedman put inside and outside the straw? _____

4 What was the result? _____

How did I do? ☆ ☆ ☆ ☆ ☆

16 **Look at page 91 of the Student's Book. Read and complete.**

> screen   disease   heat   device

1 **Kenneth Shinozuka**

What's the invention? It's a ¹_____ you put in a sock and it sends a message to a smartphone app when you stand up.

What's the invention used for? It's used for finding people with Alzheimer's ²_____.

2 **Boyan Slat**

What's the invention? It's a ³_____ using the ocean's natural currents.

What's the invention used for? It's used to catch floating plastic garbage in the ocean.

3 **Ann Makosinski**

What's the invention? It's a flashlight that gets its power from body ⁴_____.

What's the invention used for? It's used to see in the dark and it doesn't need batteries.

17 **Look at 16. Match the pictures with the inventions.**

a

b

c

18 **Design an invention. Write and draw.**

What's the invention? _____

What's the invention used for? It's used _____

Name of invention: _____

How did I do? ☆☆☆☆☆

When you write a description of an object, it's good to write about:

• the way it looks (*It's red, large, and round. It looks like an elephant's trunk.*)
• the things it has and can do (*It has two legs. It can go very fast.*)
• what it's used for (*It's used to carry heavy things.*)

Include as much information as you can so the readers can see a picture of that object in their mind.

19 Read this paragraph about an amazing object. What is it?

This object is really amazing. It's rectangular. It's white or black, with a large screen on one side. It looks like a thin book, but you can't open or close it. You can carry it everywhere in your bag. You can read and listen to music on it. It has a camera, so you can take pictures and even videos with it. You can also send and receive emails on it. It's used to entertain people on long trips. It's a _____.

20 <u>Underline</u> the sentences in **19** that describe what the object looks like. (Circle) the sentences that describe the things it has/can do. <u>Underline</u> twice the things it is used for.

21 Think of an invention. Complete the chart.

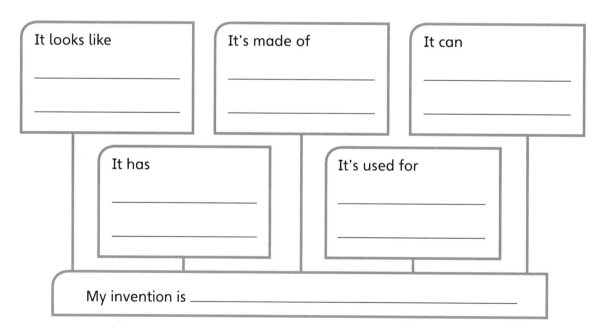

It looks like	It's made of	It can
_____	_____	_____
_____	_____	_____

It has	It's used for
_____	_____
_____	_____

My invention is _____

22 Use your chart in **21** to write a description of your invention.

How did I do? ☆☆☆☆☆

Review

23 Look at the code. Write the words. Then match the words with the pictures. Write the numbers.

●	▲	■	▬	✦	◈	⋀	⋁	➤	◄	=	+	÷
a	b	c	d	e	f	g	h	i	j	k	l	m

✗	○	◇	▢	▭	✳	!	]	?	#	%	▼	◣
n	o	p	q	r	s	t	u	v	w	x	y	z

1   # ➤ ▭ ✦ + ✦ ✳ ✳   ⋁ ✦ ● ▬ ✳ ✦ !

___ ___ ___ ___ ___ ___ ___ ___   ___ ___ ___ ___ ___ ___ ___   a ___

2   ➤ ✗ ✳ ! ● ✗ !   ■ ● ÷ ✦ ▭ ●

___ ___ ___ ___ ___ ___ ___   ___ ___ ___ ___ ___ ___   b ___

3   ▭ ● ▬ ➤ ○

___ ___ ___ ___ ___   c ___

24 Complete the dialogs. Use **used to** and **used for** and the words from the box.

> keeping shoes on   listen to music   play video games

1 A: These are headphones.

   B: _____?

   A: They're _____.

2 A: This was a games console.

   B: _____?

   A: It was _____.

3 A: These are shoelaces.

   B: _____?

   A: They're _____.

How did I do? ☆ ☆ ☆ ☆ ☆

8 Where Do They Come From?

Language in Context

1 Look at the pictures. Read about the inventions that come from these places. Do any surprise you?

1

Italy: eyeglasses, radio, piano

2

India: chess, ink, pajamas

3

England: jigsaw puzzle, matches, combustion engine

4

China: sunglasses, noodles, paper lantern

2 Circle the inventions that you use or see every day.

jigsaw puzzle	chess	matches	eyeglasses
combustion engine	ink	pajamas	piano
noodles	radio	chess	sunglasses

3 Look at 1 and 2. Where do most of the items that you circled come from?

Most of the products that I use or see were invented in _____.

4 What items that you use every day were invented in your country?

_____

5 Read. Circle two correct answers for each sentence.

1 These are made mostly of metal.

  a silver earrings   **b** planes   **c** baseballs

2 These are made of rubber.

  a kitchen gloves   **b** T-shirts   **c** rain boots

3 Some of these are made of wool.

  a cola cans   **b** blankets   **c** sweaters

4 Some of these are made of cotton.

  a T-shirts   **b** jackets   **c** tires

5 These are made of clay.

  a cups   **b** blankets   **c** plates

 119

6 Listen. What are the things? Number them in the order you hear them. Then write the names.

| balls | clothes | teacup | plane |

☐ _____

☐ _____

☐ _____

☐ _____

 **THINK BIG**

Clothes are made of a lot of different materials. Which materials can keep us warm? Which material can keep us dry?

_____

How did I do? ☆☆☆☆☆

7 Listen and read. Then answer the questions.

beach_boy

My family is planning a vacation this year. I want to go somewhere warm and sunny. I'd love to spend a lot of time on a beautiful sandy beach. Hiking would be fun, too. Where should we go?

travel_tracy

Go to the island of Korčula, one of the islands in Croatia. Fun things to do and see can be found everywhere, and it's easy to visit other islands, too. Korčula is known for its beautiful beaches and wonderful summer weather, but there are also places to go hiking and biking. Take time to walk around the historic fortified town of Korčula and photograph the amazing scenery. Go on a boat trip to the neighboring islands and enjoy eating fresh seafood, too. You'll definitely enjoy a vacation on this great island!

1 Where is Korčula?

_____

2 What's Korčula known for?

_____

3 What's special about the town?

_____

4 What two things would you like to do on Korčula? Why?

_____

_____

_____

How did I do? ☆ ☆ ☆ ☆ ☆

Language in Action

124

8 Listen. Circle **T** for true or **F** for false.

Suzy: Maybe I can find something for my sister here. Her birthday is next week.

Regina: I think you can. That table over there has <u>a bunch of handmade</u> cotton blouses. They're made in Hungary.

Suzy: They're beautiful.

Regina: Look, Margit is wearing one. See how it's worn? The strings are pulled and tied in the front. It's a nice look.

Suzy: My sister would love it! But look, the one that I like is torn.

Regina: I'm sure it can be fixed. Like the sign says, "These are all <u>gently used</u> clothes." Let's ask Margit's mother if it can be repaired.

Suzy: Great idea!

1 It's Suzy's mother's birthday soon.   T   F

2 Regina likes the blouses.   T   F

3 Suzy thinks her sister will like the blouse.   T   F

4 The blouse Suzy likes is new.   T   F

9 Look at **8**. Read the underlined expressions. Match the expressions with their meaning. Write the letters.

___ **1** a bunch of

___ **2** handmade

___ **3** gently used

a worn for a little while and still in good condition

b a lot of

c made by using your hands and not by using factory machines

10 Complete with the expressions in **9**.

A: Look at these amazing scarves. Why are they so cheap?

B: I guess it's because they're all ¹_____. But they look new.

A: I'm going to buy the red and yellow one.

B: I love this local craft fair. ²_____ these things look ³_____.

A: I know. I love things that are made by hand.

How did I do?

That rug **is made** of wool.
Those bananas **are grown** in Ecuador.

The first tire **was invented** in the U.K.
The first cola cans **were sold** in the U.S.

11 **Match the three forms of the verbs. Draw lines.**

Present Simple	Past Simple	Past Participle
eat	flew	flown
fly	made	invented
grow	ate	raised
introduce	invented	grown
invent	mined	eaten
produce	introduced	made
make	produced	introduced
mine	raised	mined
raise	grew	produced

12 **Write the sentences. Use the present simple passive form of the verbs in parentheses.**

1 Corn _____ (grow / in the U.S.).

2 Sheep _____ (raise / in New Zealand).

3 Many cars _____ (make / in China).

4 Gold _____ (mine / in South Africa).

5 Denim _____ (produce / in many countries).

6 Basketball _____ (create / in Canada).

7 The shopping cart _____ (invent / in the U.S.).

How did I do? ☆ ☆ ☆ ☆ ☆

13 **Look and complete the sentences. Use the past simple passive form of the verbs in parentheses.**

1   Chess _____ probably _____ (invent) in India.

2   In 1783, the first hot air balloon _____ (fly).

3   The first shopping cart _____ (make) in 1937.

4   The phonograph, or record player, _____ (introduce) in 1877 by Thomas Edison.

14 **Unscramble the words. Use them to write sentences. Use the present simple passive form of the verb.**

1   acrs   rpudeco

    *cars*_____   *produce*_____

    *Cars are produced*_____ in Brazil.

2   ldgo   niem

    _____   _____

    _____ in Peru.

3   sehcs   lypa

    _____   _____

    _____ all over the world.

4   tobos   emka

    _____   _____

    _____ of rubber.

How did I do? ☆ ☆ ☆ ☆ ☆

15 **Match the words with the definitions. Write the letters.**

___ **1** fresh produce

a something that has a harmful effect on air, land, or water

___ **2** pollution

b foodstuffs that go bad quickly

___ **3** imported

c usual or normal

___ **4** country of origin

d brought from a different country

___ **5** typical

e where something or someone comes from

126

16 **Read and complete with the words from the box. Then listen and check.**

distribution center   fresh   local   pollution   typical

Farmers' Markets and Our Future

Where does your family buy fresh fruit and vegetables from? Do you go to a supermarket or do you go to a farmers' market? All over the world, farmers gather on specific days in specific places, like a park or parking lot, to sell their produce directly to customers. Their produce is fresh – often picked just the day before! It's also seasonal, which means that in the summer you can buy only summer fruits and vegetables, and in the winter you can buy only winter fruits and vegetables. Some farmers' markets also have live entertainment, like singers and musicians, and sell things other than produce, like crafts made by ¹_____ people. So they can be a great place to find and buy gifts for people and just to have fun!

Shopping at a farmers' market can be a good thing to do. Here's why:

A   You can meet local farmers and learn about their produce. You can find out what's in season, and some farmers may give advice on how to prepare and cook their produce.

B   Locally-grown food is very ²_____. It hasn't been stored or refrigerated for long, and it hasn't been transported far. So every bite tastes good!

C   The food doesn't have to travel a long distance from the farm to a ³_____ and then to you. It goes only a short distance from the farm to you. This results in less ⁴_____ and helps keep the environment clean.

D   Buying from local farmers can help the environment in other ways, too. When farmers don't make enough money to live on, they are often obliged to sell their farms to land developers. The developers build houses and buildings on the farmland. More houses may cause more pollution and greater demands on natural resources like rivers, lakes, and forests in the area.

E   A ⁵_____ farm is a beautiful place. It has fields, meadows, woods, and ponds. It provides homes for animals like rabbits, birds, and deer. So if the farm disappears, the animals may have nowhere to live, and you may have nowhere to go to enjoy nature's beauty.

Next time your mom buys vegetables, think about asking her to go to a local farmers' market. You'll have a fun time, and you'll support your local community.

How did I do? ☆☆☆☆☆

128

17 **Read and complete. Then listen and check.**

machine	school	problem	useful	invent

Problems and Inventions

1 All over the world, there are objects that people use and things people do which have been invented. Why do people ¹_____ things? Where do ideas for inventions come from? There's a saying that, "Necessity is the mother of invention." This means that people invent things because there's a problem, and they want to solve the problem.

2 In 1912, American engineer Otto Frederick Rohwedder had an idea. He wanted to invent a ²_____ that could slice a whole loaf of bread. He built his first bread slicer in 1917, but it was destroyed in a fire. In 1927, he had enough money to build another one. But he realized he had a ³_____ – the bread became stale after it was cut. He then had another idea, and he built a bread slicer that sliced the bread and then wrapped it so that it wouldn't get stale so quickly. So the next time you see a loaf of sliced bread, think about Otto Frederick Rohwedder's invention and how ⁴_____ it is to us every day!

3 Society needs inventors. Our lives are better because inventors are problem-solvers. Many of them solve everyday problems by inventing something useful. Think of a problem in your home or at your ⁵_____. Can you invent something to solve it?

18 **Read 17 again and answer the questions.**

1 What did Otto Frederick Rohwedder invent?

_____

2 What problem did he have?

_____

3 How did he solve the problem?

_____

4 When did he build his first bread slicer?

_____

How did I do? ☆☆☆☆☆

When you write a persuasive paragraph, you want your reader to agree with your opinion. A good persuasive paragraph gives a strong main opinion and reasons for that opinion. Your reasons make your opinion stronger and more believable.

Opinion: *The South of France is a perfect place for a vacation.*

Reasons: *It has beautiful beaches with wonderful swimming and nice scenery.*

There are wonderful street markets, and the local food is delicious.

There are interesting and historic towns to visit, too, such as Nice and Montpellier.

19 **Read the persuasive paragraph. Then answer the questions.**

¹Cape Town is famous all over the world because it's a wonderful vacation destination. It's located at the tip of Africa in South Africa. ²You won't be bored here because there are lots of fun things to do. ³You can swim and sunbathe at Camps Bay, a favorite beach, and you can surf here, too. ⁴You can go on bus tours around the city, or boat tours to see dolphins, seals, and humpback whales. ⁵You can also hike up Table Mountain, or go up in a cable car. The view from the top is amazing! ⁶Cape Town is full of wonderful adventures for everyone. Why not choose it for your next vacation?

1 Which sentence is the main opinion? _____

2 How many reasons are given for that opinion? _____

3 Which sentences are the reasons? _____

4 Do you want to go there? Why/Why not? _____

20 **Think of a nice vacation spot.**
Complete the chart with your ideas.

Give a reason.
_____

Name the vacation spot.
_____
_____

Give your opinion.
_____
_____

Give a second reason.
_____

Give a third reason.
_____

21 **Use your chart in 20 to write a persuasive paragraph about your vacation spot.**

How did I do? ☆ ☆ ☆ ☆ ☆

Review

22 **Circle the products that are made of the materials in the chart.**

Wool	Rubber	Cotton	Metal	Clay
rug	tire	plate	oven	sweater
scarf	boots	towels	cola can	plate
cola can	paper	T-shirt	floor	bowls
blanket	eraser	plane	food	flower pot

23 **Read and circle the correct answers.**

1 Coffee ___ in Costa Rica and you can visit coffee farms there.

  a was grown   **b** is grown

2 Beautiful glass ___ in Italy. You can buy it in fancy stores.

  a was made   **b** is made

3 Bar codes ___ in the U.S. long ago.

  a were invented   **b** are invented

4 Fantastic watches ___ in Switzerland and stores all over the world sell them.

  a are made   **b** were made

5 A lot of cattle ___ in Argentina today.

  a were raised   **b** are raised

6 The jigsaw puzzle ___ by an Englishman in 1767.

  a was invented   **b** is invented

24 **Complete the sentences with the correct form of the verbs in parentheses.**

1 Jars _____ (make) from glass.

2 Apples _____ (grow) in New York State and are very popular in the fall.

3 The modern safety pin _____ (invent) in the U.S. in 1849.

4 The earliest noodles _____ (eat) in China a long, long time ago.

How did I do? ☆☆☆☆☆

9 How Adventurous Are You?

Language in Context

 133

1 Listen and match. Write the number.

a

b

c

d

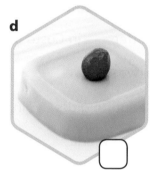

2 Read about the food in the pictures in **1**. Rate them. **1** = I really want to try it!
2 = I might want to try it. **3** = I never want to try it!

1 This Filipino dessert is called Buko Pandan. It looks pretty, and it has a wonderful sweet taste. ___

2 Tandoori chicken is a popular traditional dish from India. It is made with chicken and spices like pepper and curry. It tastes hot and spicy! ___

3 Chinese soup has tofu in it. It's hot and sour. It has a very unusual taste! ___

4 Marinated octopus is a traditional seafood dish from Greece. The octopus is left in olive oil, lemon juice, and herbs for a short time. It's delicious! ___

3 How adventurous are you with food? Look at your ratings in **2** and ✓ your answer.

☐ I'm very adventurous. I rated most of the food as **1**.

☐ I'm somewhat adventurous. I rated most of the food as **2**.

☐ I'm not adventurous at all. I rated most of the food as **3**.

4 Listen and ✓ the words you hear for each food.

	unusual	tasty	popular	raw	spicy	sweet	traditional	delicious
1 gazpacho								
2 sushi								
3 tagine								
4 spumoni								

5 What food do you like? What food don't you like? What does it taste like?

_____

_____

THINK BIG

Name a traditional food from your country. Then circle words to describe it.

_____

hot / raw / sweet / spicy / cold / sour
unusual / popular / delicious

How did I do? ☆ ☆ ☆ ☆ ☆

6 Listen and read. Then answer the questions.

Life on a Boat

Eleven-year-old Glenn Dodd has lived on a boat with his family for the past two years. A local radio station is interviewing him.

Interviewer: Today on Awesome Adventures, we're talking to eleven-year-old Glenn Dodd. Glenn's family has lived on a boat and has traveled around Australia for the last two years. Tell me, Glenn, what's it like living on a boat?

Glenn Dodd: Well, in the beginning it was really hard. There are four people in my family and a dog. The boat is small, so we were always very close to each other.

Interviewer: Wow! I'm sure that was tough sometimes.

Glenn Dodd: Yes, we had to learn to get along, or my dad said he'd throw us into the ocean!

Interviewer: That would make me behave, too! What do you like the most about life on a boat?

Glenn Dodd: Well, probably all the new things I can try.

Interviewer: Like what? Give me an example.

Glenn Dodd: Well, I've eaten alligator meat a few times. And I've scuba dived with stingrays. That was a little scary!

Interviewer: I can imagine it was! Now tell me, after two years, would you rather live on a boat or in a house?

Glenn Dodd: Honestly, I really want to live in a house now, like my friends. Actually, my family has decided to go back home next month. So, soon, I'm going to be a land creature again.

Interviewer: Well, good luck, Glenn. That's all the time we have. Thanks again for sharing your story.

1 Where does Glenn Dodd live now? _____

2 What does he like most about living there? _____

3 Do you think Glenn is an adventurous person? Why/Why not? _____

_____

How did I do? ☆ ☆ ☆ ☆ ☆

Language in Action

7 Listen. Then circle the correct answers.

Allie: Hi, Roberto. Let's <u>do something</u> on Saturday afternoon.

Roberto: <u>That sounds good,</u> Allie. But I have a lesson on Saturday.

Allie: You have lessons on Saturdays?

Roberto: Yes. I'm learning Chinese!

Allie: Chinese? Really?

Roberto: Yes. It's really interesting. Have you ever studied another language?

Allie: Well, I can speak English and Spanish. But I've never studied another language.

Roberto: It's a lot of fun. And I'm learning a lot. I can say so many things in Chinese already.

Allie: <u>That's amazing!</u> How do you say *hello* in Chinese?

Roberto: Ni hao, Allie!

Allie: Hola, Roberto!

1 Roberto and Allie are   **a** friends.   **b** brother and sister.

2 Roberto studies Chinese on   **a** Sundays.   **b** Saturdays.

3 Allie speaks   **a** English and Chinese.   **b** English and Spanish.

4 Roberto   **a** enjoys studying Chinese.   **b** doesn't like studying Chinese.

5 *Ni hao* means   **a** 'goodbye'.   **b** 'hello'.

8 Look at 7. Read the underlined expressions. Match the expressions with their meanings. Write the letters.

___ **1** do something   **a** Wow! That's great!

___ **2** That sounds good.   **b** go somewhere and have fun

___ **3** That's amazing!   **c** That's a good idea.

9 Complete with the expressions in 8.

A: Hi, Jack. Do you want to ¹_____ on Sunday afternoon?

B: ²_____. Do you want to go to the movies? I have two tickets, and they were free!

A: ³_____. Where did you get them from?

B: They were a present.

How did I do? ☆☆☆☆☆

Grammar

> **Have** you **ever been** to a concert?   Yes, I **have.**/No, I **haven't.**
>
> **Has** he **ever been** skydiving?   Yes, he **has.**/No, he **hasn't.**

10 Match the three forms of the verbs. Draw lines.

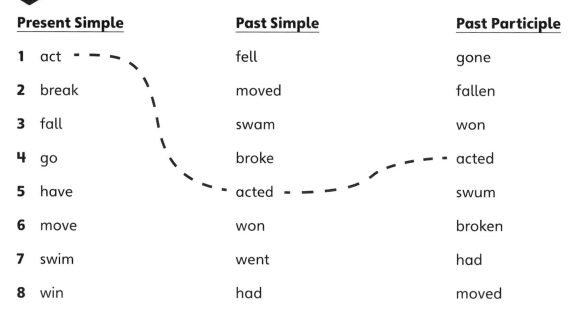

Present Simple	Past Simple	Past Participle
1 act	fell	gone
2 break	moved	fallen
3 fall	swam	won
4 go	broke	acted
5 have	acted	swum
6 move	won	broken
7 swim	went	had
8 win	had	moved

11 Unscramble the questions. Then look and write the answers.

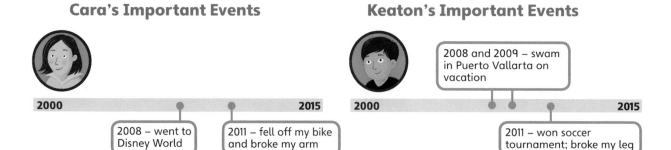

Cara's Important Events

2000   2015

2008 – went to Disney World

2011 – fell off my bike and broke my arm

Keaton's Important Events

2008 and 2009 – swam in Puerto Vallarta on vacation

2000   2015

2011 – won soccer tournament; broke my leg

1 ever / has / been / Cara / to Disney World?

_____

_____

2 Cara / swum / ever / has / in Puerto Vallarta?

_____

_____

3 Keaton / has / been / to Puerto Vallarta / ever?

_____

_____

4 Keaton / broken / his arm / has / ever?

_____

_____

How did I do? ☆ ☆ ☆ ☆ ☆

Would they **rather** play soccer or watch it?   They'**d rather** play soccer.

> **I'd** = I would
> **you'd** = you would
> **he'd** = he would
> **she'd** = she would
> **they'd** = they would

12   Follow the lines. Make guesses and answer the questions.

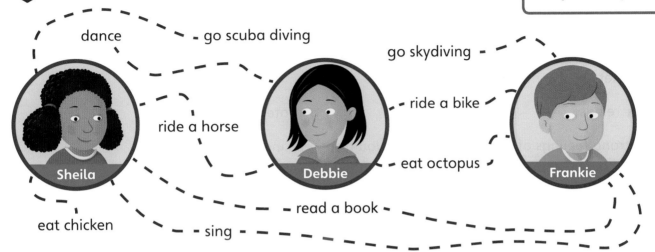

1   Would Sheila rather go skydiving or go scuba diving?

   She'd rather go scuba diving.

2   Would Sheila and Debbie rather ride a bike or ride a horse?

   _____

3   Would Frankie and Debbie rather eat chicken or eat octopus?

   _____

4   Would Frankie and Sheila rather watch cartoons or read a book?

   _____

13   **Answer the questions.**

1   Would you rather eat chicken or eat octopus?

   _____

2   Would you rather ride a bike or ride a horse?

   _____

3   Would you rather go skydiving or go scuba diving?

   _____

How did I do?

14 **Read and circle the correct answers.**

1   A chemical that your body produces when you are excited, frightened, or angry.

    a adrenal glands   **b** adrenalin

2   A chemical which your body produces that affects your body.

    a hormone   **b** oxygen

3   To let go of something (or someone).

    a release   **b** protect

4   Strong feelings of worry that prevent you from relaxing.

    a boost   **b** stress

5   The smallest part of a living thing.

    a oxygen   **b** cell

15 **Listen and read. Then circle T for true or F for false.**

Extreme Sports

Many people exercise to relax and to release stress. But other people like sports that are exciting and may even be dangerous like motorcar racing, skiing, and rock climbing. These people love the feel of adrenalin rushing through their bodies, giving them that extra boost of energy. The sudden boost of this hormone is called an adrenalin rush.

Freeriding

Freeriding is like big wave surfing on snow. Skiers go to the top of a very high, steep mountain and ski down it. There are no paths for them to follow – they just follow the natural paths down the mountain. Where does the adrenalin rush come from? They go down the mountain very, very fast because the slopes that they ski down are very steep. Some slopes are almost at 90 degrees to the ground. They also fly in the air in some places, over rock-covered snow cliffs. Now that sounds very exciting, doesn't it?

1   Some extreme sports can give people an adrenalin rush.   T   F

2   Freeriders ski down very high, steep mountains.   T   F

3   Freeriders follow a path.   T   F

4   Freeriders aren't adventurous.   T   F

144

16 **Read and complete. Then listen and check.**

| achieved | extreme sports | goals | professional | risks | sail |

Record-breaking Teenagers

All around the world, there are teenagers who do amazing things at home, at school, or on the sports field. But some teenagers take enormous ¹_____ and break records in the world of ²_____. Let's read about two record-breaking teenagers, who set out to achieve and succeed in reaching their amazing ³_____.

Jordan Romero is a ⁴_____ climber who, as a teenager, climbed seven of the highest and most challenging mountains on seven continents. He climbed his first mountain, Mount Kilimanjaro in Africa, in 2006, when he was ten years old. He's the youngest person in the world to do this. In 2011, when he was fifteen years old, he climbed the last of the seven mountains, a mountain in Antarctica. Jordan, who lives in California, wants to help other teenagers reach their goals, so he started a group called Find Your Everest.

In 2012, a Dutch teenager, Laura Dekker, became the youngest person to ⁵_____ around the world on her own. Laura has been on or near water all her life. She was born on a boat, got her first boat when she was six years old, and at eight years old began dreaming about sailing around the world. At ten years old, she got her second boat, *Guppy*, and at fifteen years old she set off on her long trip. A year and a day later, she ⁶_____ her goal. She was just sixteen years old. When Laura finished the trip and got off her boat, her mother, father, sister, grandparents, and many cheering fans greeted her.

17 **Read 16 again and answer the questions.**

1 How many mountains on how many continents has Jordan Romero climbed?

_____

2 How old was Jordan when he climbed his last mountain?

_____

3 What does Find Your Everest do?

_____

4 How old was Laura when she got her first boat?

_____

5 How old was Laura when she set off to achieve her goal?

_____

How did I do? ☆ ☆ ☆ ☆ ☆

A good description includes:

- a clear topic sentence that tells the reader what you are going to write about. (*I'm not a risk-taker.*)
- more information about the topic that gives examples or details. You can introduce your examples using *For example*. Always use a comma. (*For example, I don't like trying new foods. I also get nervous when I go to new places where I can't speak the language.*)
- a summary that retells your topic sentence in a new way. (*It's OK that I'm not a risk-taker because it's good to have different people in the world.*)

18 **Read the description. Then answer the questions. Write the numbers.**

> ¹I'm not at all adventurous, and I don't like to try new things. ²For example, I don't play sports because every time I've played, I've gotten hurt. ³I also don't like trying new foods, and I prefer to eat the same food every day. ⁴This is strange because my whole family loves trying food from different cultures. ⁵Everyone says I should be more adventurous and try new things, but I'm happy just the way I am.

___ **1**   Which sentence is the topic sentence?

___ **2**   Which sentences give details about the topic?

___ **3**   Which sentence retells the topic in a new way?

19 **Think of ways that you are not adventurous. Complete the chart.**

Complete the sentence: *I am not adventurous because…*
Give an example and details.
Give another example and details.
Write a summary. Explain in one sentence how you are not adventurous.

20 **Write a paragraph about how you are not adventurous. Use 19 to help you.**

How did I do? ☆ ☆ ☆ ☆ ☆

21 **Find and circle these words.**

popular
raw
sour
spicy
sweet
tasty
traditional
unusual

```
              q  z  i  w
        a  x  c  b  w  j  t  k
        n  o  m  v  d  q  y  r  f  d
        u  d  p  z  p  a  r  a  w  s
     a  n  s  o  u  r  g  h  d  i  a  m
     i  u  m  p  m  r  s  p  i  c  y  n
     l  s  f  u  b  l  w  g  t  p  z  b
     q  u  p  l  x  y  e  f  i  j  n  v
     a  a  e  a  g  l  e  d  o  t  e  c
        l  q  r  w  q  t  s  n  y  u  s
           t  a  s  t  y  a  a  s  y
              i  m  v  l  j  l
```

22 **Complete the sentences. Use some of the words in 21.**

1 One soup at the Spanish restaurant has a lot of spices in it. Not many people order it.

The soup is too _____ so it isn't _____.

2 Many of the dishes at the Greek restaurant are delicious seafood dishes. One of the dishes is eaten by everyone in Greece and was eaten long ago, too.

That seafood dish is _____ and _____.

3 The new Mexican restaurant has a dessert that is made with avocado and lime.

The avocado dessert isn't common. It's _____. It isn't sweet like usual desserts.
It's _____.

23 **Complete the questions. Use the correct form of the words in parentheses. Then answer the questions about yourself.**

1 _____ you ever_____ (go) to a Japanese restaurant?

_____

2 _____ you ever _____ (see) an octopus?

_____

3 _____ you ever _____ (eat) grasshoppers?

_____

How did I do? ☆ ☆ ☆ ☆ ☆

1 Unscramble and write the words. Add your own words on the extra lines.

Gadgets

1 _____
2 _____
3 _____
4 _____
5 _____

1 nattisn aecamr

2 llce onhpe

3 welresis hadeest

4 agmes onclsoe

Products and Materials

1 _____
2 _____
3 _____
4 _____

1 tootnc

2 bankltes

3 yacl

1 edusoiilc

2 lpruapo

3 tadiilnroat

4 uusulan

Food

1 _____
2 _____
3 _____
4 _____
5 _____

2 **Find a song that talks about gadgets, products, and materials, or food. Complete the chart about the song.**

Song title	
Who's the singer?	
Where does the singer come from?	
Who was the song written by?	
What's your favorite line in the song? Why?	
Would the singer rather sing traditional songs or popular songs?	
Has the song ever been a number one hit?	
Who else do you think might sing the song well?	

3 **Write a note to your parents. Persuade them to let you go to a concert to hear this song and singer. Use the information in 2 to help you.**

_____

_____

_____

_____

_____

_____

_____

_____

_____

Extra Grammar Practice

1 Read about Lisa and Dan. Choose the correct verb and use it in the correct form to complete the sentences.

"I'm in the drama club. I play the trumpet in the school orchestra. I can draw, but I can't paint. Soccer is fun, but basketball is boring."

Lisa

"I'm in the math club. I want to learn how to do martial arts. Soccer is fun, but basketball isn't fun. I can't draw."

Dan

1 Lisa is good at _____ (draw/paint).

2 Dan is interested in _____ (act/do martial arts).

3 They aren't interested in _____ (draw/play basketball).

4 They enjoy _____ (play soccer/play basketball).

2 Look at 1. Complete the sentences with the correct form of the words in parentheses.

1 Lisa _____ (good at/paint).

2 Dan _____ (enjoy/draw).

3 Dan _____ (like/do math).

4 Lisa _____ (love/play the trumpet).

3 Look at 1 and complete the dialogs. Use the words in parentheses and any other words necessary.

1 **Lisa:** How about joining the art club?

 Dan: No, thanks. I _____ (good at).

2 **Dan:** Do you want to join the math club?

 Lisa: I don't think so. I _____ (interested in).

3 **Emily:** How about joining the soccer club?

 Dan and Lisa: Why not? We _____ (love).

4 **Brian:** Why don't you try out for the basketball team?

 Dan and Lisa: Definitely not! We _____ (enjoy).

How did I do? ☆☆☆☆☆

Extra Grammar Practice

1 **Complete the sentences. Use the correct form of the verbs in parentheses.**

1

My parents _____ (get married) when they _____ (be) very young. A few months later, they _____ (move) to London.

2

My father _____ (open) his own restaurant in Brighton when I _____ (be) a teenager. I _____ (work) with my father every weekend. A few years ago, I _____ (help) my father open his second restaurant.

2 **Read and draw the pictures. Then write the answers.**

1 Alice is shorter than Carl. Barbara is taller than Alice but shorter than Carl.

Who's the tallest?

_____

2 Jose is younger than Frank. Frank is older than Edward. Edward is older than Jose.

Who's the youngest?

_____

3 My brother, Ted, is very strong. He's stronger than my dad. My dad is stronger than my mom. I'm Mark. I'm stronger than Ted.

Who's the strongest in the family?

_____

How did I do? ☆☆☆☆☆

Extra Grammar Practice

1 How could students help their school? Make suggestions. Use **could** and the words from the box.

> clean up the playground   paint the art room   plant trees

1 Sophia _____

_____

2 Brian _____

_____

3 Jilly _____

_____

2 Unscramble the words. Then write sentences with **am going to, is going to,** or **are going to.** What are these students going to do this week?

1 shaw arsc   We _____.

_____

2 rweti alteircs   Peter and Jake _____.

_____

3 acek slae   I _____.

_____

4 eakm sptrseo   Rebecca _____.

_____

How did I do? ☆ ☆ ☆ ☆ ☆

Extra Grammar Practice

1 **Look at the chart. Complete the sentences. Use more/less ... than or the least/the most and the words in parentheses.**

	Jeff	Tony	Silvia
Making a volcano	👍👍	👍👍	👍
Mixing liquids	👍	👍	👍👍
Making electricity	👍👍👍	👍👍	👍👍👍

How did the students feel about their science class experiments?

1 **Silvia:** Mixing liquids was _____ (interesting) making a volcano.

2 **Jeff:** Making electricity was _____ (exciting) of all.

3 **Tony:** Mixing liquids was _____ (amazing) experiment.

4 **Jeff:** Making a volcano was _____ (challenging) making electricity.

2 **Look at 1. Write sentences. Use as ... as or not as ... as.**

1 **Jeff:** making a volcano / fun / making electricity

_____

2 **Tony:** making electricity / exciting / making a volcano

_____

3 **Silvia:** mixing liquids / interesting / making electricity

_____

3 **Look at 1. Write sentences. Use too or not enough and the words in parentheses.**

1 **Silvia:** I didn't like making a volcano. It was _____ (interesting).

2 **Jeff:** Mixing liquids wasn't fun. It was _____ (boring).

3 **Tony:** I'm not interested in mixing liquids. It was _____ (exciting).

How did I do? ☆☆☆☆☆

Extra Grammar Practice

1 **Match the puzzle pieces. Then answer the questions.**

1 What was Charlie doing when he got sunburned?

_____

2 What happened while James and Dan were skiing?

_____

3 What were Alison and Jo doing when they got lost?

_____

4 What happened while Ellie was biking?

_____

2 **Look at 1. Answer the questions.**

1 Was Charlie camping when he got sunburned?

_____

2 Were James and Dan swimming when they got hurt?

_____

3 Were Alison and Jo hiking when they got lost?

_____

4 Was Ellie rafting when she got wet?

_____

How did I do? ☆ ☆ ☆ ☆ ☆

Extra Grammar Practice

1   **Read. Then complete the sentences. Use no one and everyone.**

100 years from now, the world will be very different. **1**_____ will use smartphones because our phones will be inside our heads! **2**_____ will use flying cars, and **3**_____ will live in apartments in tall buildings in space. Not like today. Today, many people live in houses. In the future, **4**_____ will live in houses any more. Machines will make our food at home and in restaurants. **5**_____ will need to cook any more. **6**_____ will study in schools because there won't be any school buildings, and we won't have teachers. **7**_____ will study at home using computers.

2   **Look at 1. Complete the sentences. Use will or won't and the verbs in parentheses.**

1   There _____ (be) any teachers.

2   We _____ (call) people with cell phones.

3   We _____ (live) in apartments in space.

4   People _____ (drive) flying cars.

5   We _____ (cook). Machines _____ (cook) for us.

3   **Match the sentences. Write the letters.**

In the future…

___ **1**   Students won't need teachers.

___ **2**   We'll go to the moon on vacation.

___ **3**   No one will go to friends' houses.

___ **4**   Everyone will be happy.

a   We'll meet by video messaging.

b   They'll teach themselves.

c   Nobody will be sad.

d   Space travel will be cheap.

4   **Look at 3. Do you think these things will happen? Write your answers.**

_____

_____

How did I do? ☆☆☆☆☆

Extra Grammar Practice

1   **Complete the sentences. Use is/are used to and the words from the box.**

> eat   get around   protect eyes   write

1   A pencil _____.

2   Plates _____.

3   A bike _____.

4   Sunglasses _____.

2   **Complete the sentences. Use was/were used for and the words in parentheses.**

1   This instant camera is from 1974.

It _____ (take/pictures).

2   These radios are from 1956.

They _____ (listen/to music).

3   This cell phone is from 1982.

It _____ (talk/to people).

4   These games consoles are from 1990.

They _____ (play/video games).

3   **Answer the questions. Use the words in parentheses.**

1   I'm thinking of something. It's round and it bounces. People play a game with it. What do you think it is?

_____ (may)

2   I'm thinking of a type of sweet food. They're small and taste nice. They're often seen at birthday parties. What do you think they are?

_____ (might)

3   I'm thinking of a small insect. It likes hot, wet weather. It can fly, and it makes a noise when it flies. What do you think it is?

_____ (might)

     How did I do? ☆☆☆☆☆

Extra Grammar Practice

1   **Complete the sentences. Use the correct passive form of the verbs in parentheses.**

1   The very first cookie _____ (make) in Persia.

2   Apples _____ (grow) in many countries today.

3   In 2005, a bowl of noodles 4,000 years old _____ (discover) by scientists in China.

4   Bananas _____ (pick) in the Caribbean every year.

5   A lot of coffee _____ (produce) in Colombia these days.

2   **Complete the puzzle. Write the letters. Use the words from the box.**

Africa	Argentina	Brazil	China
invent	mine	produce	raise

1

A _ _ _ _ _ _
d i a m o n d s
_ _ _

2

A _ _ _ _
r _
c a t t l e
_ _ _ _ _

3

C _ _ _ i _ _
n o o d l e s
_ _ _ _
_

4

i _
B _ _ _ p
r u b b e r
_ _ _ _ _ _

3   **Look at 2. Write sentences. Use is/are or was/were and the words in the puzzle.**

1 _____

2 _____

3 _____

4 _____

How did I do? ☆☆☆☆☆

Extra Grammar Practice

1   **Look at the chart. Complete and answer the questions.**

	fly to the U.K.	win a spelling quiz	ride a horse	visit China	eat octopus
Georgina	✓			✓	✓
Rob		✓	✓		✓

1   _____ Georgina ever _____ to the U.K.?

_____

2   _____ Georgina ever _____ a spelling quiz?

_____

3   _____ Georgina ever _____ China?

_____

4   _____ Rob ever _____ octopus?

_____

5   _____ Rob ever _____ a horse?

_____

Georgina

Rob

2   **Read. Then complete and answer the questions. Use would rather.**

Tom and Sara like spicy food, adventurous sports, beaches, and adrenalin rushes. Karen likes unusual food, but she doesn't like spicy food, scary sports, mountains, or adrenalin rushes.

1   _____ Karen _____ eat spicy food or an avocado dessert?

_____

2   _____ Tom and Sara _____ visit a museum or ski down a mountain?

_____

3   _____ Sara _____ go swimming or mountain climbing?

_____

4   _____ Tom and Sara _____ ride a motorcycle fast or slowly?

_____

How did I do? ☆ ☆ ☆ ☆ ☆

Pearson Education Limited
KAO Two
KAO Park
Harlow
Essex
CM17 9NA
England
and Associated Companies throughout the world.

www.pearsonelt.com/bigenglish2

First published 2017
Fourteenth impression 2024

ISBN: 978-1-2922-3334-5

Set in Heinemann Roman
Printed in Slovakia by Neografia

Acknowledgements
The publisher would like to thank the following for their kind permission to reproduce their photographs:

(Key: b-bottom; c-centre; l-left; r-right; t-top)

123RF.com: 8l, alexeysmirnov 72t, Arina Zaiachin 70/3, Gennadiy Poznyakov 2 (b), Jiri Vaclavek 66/2, joseelias 72c, Susan Leggett 3, 11br, 32t/4, Oleg Mikhaylov 2 (c), photobac 73 (c), Rick Sargeant 2 (f), scanrail 11cr, Wittaya Puangkingkaew 85; **Alamy Stock Photo:** AF Archive 93b, age fotostock 61, Frankie Angel 67/2, 68t, Blend Images 22/4, 100b/4, Jonah Calinawan 87/3, Mark Conlin 18l, Corepics 64c/4, Hilda DeSanctis 71/3, Judy Freilicher 11tl, Granger Historical Picture Archive 69, Ruth Hofshi 18tr, Hugh Threlfall 66/4, Hyperstar 20, Image Source 64c/1, imageBROKER 88b, Irene Abdou 19 (c), Iain Masterton 34/5, Morgan Lane Photography 22/6, 100t/3, Keith Morris 22/5, 32b/4, pabtravel 44/6, Panther Media GmbH 49/6, Paul Springett 03 67/4, Myrleen Pearson 22/1, 49/4, Simon Price 64c/2, PRILL Mediendesign 66/3, Lana Rastro 12/4, 32c/2, 99b, RosaIreneBetancourt 10 32t/2, 100t/2, Neil Setchfield 19 (a), Sinibomb Images 22/2, 100b/1, Steve Vidler 41; **Brand X Pictures:** Burke Triolo Productions 72b; **Fotolia.com:** 2tun 43l, 64t/1, Africa Studio 64t/2, alarsonphoto 43r, Aaron Amat 67/3, asese 4b, bkhphoto 64c/3, BVDC 99t, Cybrain 8tc (right), dja65 71/1, 81tr, DM7 60c, emese73 8tl, Gelpi 4tl, GoodMood Photo 77tl, Haslam Photography 34/4, Barbara Helgason 34/3, 64t/4, Darrin Henry 2 (d), 32t/3, Herjua 5lt, higyou 60t, Ken Hurst 31/4, 45, 103, JJAVA 86 (c), JonMilnes 88t, Kadmy 12/1, 32c/1, kaphotokevm1 12/3, 32c/4, KaYann 76/1, Igor Klimov 55r, 64b/4, Mitchell Knapton 49/1, Douglas Knight 8tc (left), Robert Lerich 86 (b), MasterLu 5lb, MaszaS 44/4, mirabella 43c, Monkey Business 2 (a), 8r, 44/2, 49/5, Denis Pepin 77bl, percent 77tr, plutofrosti 55cr, 64b/2, Denys Prykhodov 55l, SerrNovik 11bl, skynet 105, soundsnaps 75t (a), strelov 68b, Milos Tasic 81 (boots), tuja66 75t (b), Tupungato 82, Simone van den Berg 22/3, 32b/3, 100b/3, EJ White 31/3, Lisa F. Young 11cl, 100b/2; **Getty Images:** Juan Camilo Bernal 73 (b left), iStock Unreleased 67/1, 75 (game boy), Maskot 29, Mlenny 32b/1, Visage / Stockbyte 19 (b); **Pearson Education Ltd:** Jon Barlow 31/1; **Shutterstock.com:** 3Dstock 64b/1, 67 (d), Aaron Amat 81 (gold), Adisa 81 (car), Alex Staroseltsev 11tr, alexnika 71/2, Tobias Arhelger 73 (a), baitong333 44/5, 49/3, bikeriderlondon 44/1, Fernando Blanco Calzada 55cl, 64b/3, 67 (b), bonchan 87/1, Boonsom 76/2, Patrick Breig 36, 60b, Norman Chan 86 (a), Hung Chung Chih 76/4, Oleksandr Chub 75t (c), clearviewstock 18br, Melanie DeFazio 12/5, djem 70/2, 75 (shoelace), Ersler Dmitry 67 (a), Michelle Eadie 93t, eurobanks 4tr, 31/2, fet 2 (e), 32t/1, Natali Glado 34/6, HomeStudio 71/4, IM_photo 92, Imagebroker.net 40, Janimal 83, Robert Kneschke 12/2, 32c/3, Susan Leggett 44/3, 49/2, LuckyPhoto 34/2, marekuliasz 34/1, 42, 64t/3, marylooo 100t/1, musicman 77br, Nata-Lia 70/1, 75 (earphones), Ociacia 66/1, Antonio V. Oquias 86 (d), Daniel Padavona 87/4, Igor Plotnikov 78, Ralko 67 (c), 70/4, rprongjai 87/2, Renata Sedmakova 76/3, Charles Taylor 56, Val Thoermer 32b/2, Tomasz Trojanowski 37, Pavel Vakhrushev 73 (b right), vblinov 81 (chess), Wallenrock 19 (d), wavebreakmedia 15, Michael Woodruff 9

Illustrated by
Zaharias Papadopoulos (Hyphen), Q2A Media Services, Anthony Lewis, Christos Skaltsas (Hyphen).

Tracklist

Class CD track number	Workbook CD track number	Unit and activity number
6	2	Unit 1, activity 1
9	3	Unit 1, activity 6
12	4	Unit 1, activity 8
13	5	Unit 1, activity 10
15	6	Unit 1, activity 17
17	7	Unit 1, activity 19
25	8	Unit 2, activity 4
27	9	Unit 2, activity 5
30	10	Unit 2, activity 7
31	11	Unit 2, activity 13
33	12	Unit 2, activity 17
35	13	Unit 2, activity 18
41	14	Unit 3, activity 4
43	15	Unit 3, activity 5
46	16	Unit 3, activity 7
48	17	Unit 3, activity 16
57	18	Unit 4, activity 4
59	19	Unit 4, activity 6
62	20	Unit 4, activity 8
64	21	Unit 4, activity 16
66	22	Unit 4, activity 17
73	23	Unit 5, activity 5
76	24	Unit 5, activity 7

Class CD track number	Workbook CD track number	Unit and activity number
78	25	Unit 5, activity 15
80	26	Unit 5, activity 17
88	27	Unit 6, activity 5
91	28	Unit 6, activity 7
92	29	Unit 6, activity 10
94	30	Unit 6, activity 15
96	31	Unit 6, activity 16
104	32	Unit 7, activity 4
106	33	Unit 7, activity 5
109	34	Unit 7, activity 7
119	35	Unit 8, activity 6
121	36	Unit 8, activity 7
124	37	Unit 8, activity 8
126	38	Unit 8, activity 16
128	39	Unit 8, activity 17
133	40	Unit 9, activity 1
135	41	Unit 9, activity 4
137	42	Unit 9, activity 6
140	43	Unit 9, activity 7
142	44	Unit 9, activity 15
144	45	Unit 9, activity 16